# SOUTH AFRICA
# 1948–1994

Rosemary Mulholland

CAMBRIDGE
UNIVERSITY PRESS

University Printing House, Cambridge CB2 8BS, United Kingdom

Cambridge University Press is part of the University of Cambridge.

It furthers the University's mission by disseminating knowledge in the pursuit of education, learning and research at the highest international levels of excellence.

www.cambridge.org
Information on this title: www.cambridge.org/9780521576789

First published 1997
8th printing 2012

*A catalogue record for this publication is available from the British Library*

ISBN 978-0-521-57678-9 Paperback

Picture research by Marilyn Rawlings

Illustrations by Gecko Limited, Bicester, Oxon

**Acknowledgements**
Cover: *Images of Defiance*, South African History Archive
Museum Africa 4; e.t. archive 5; Camera Press 6 and 21 background, 10 (Howarth), 19 (Clayton), 26t (Spencer), 38 (Berry), 42t (Berry), 43 tr (Spencer), 44 (Clayton), 53 (Sana), 54 (Van der Merwe), 55 (Kopec); Weidenfeld and Nicholson Archive 7, Mayibuye Centre 8, 9, 18, 24, 28, 36, 40, 42b, 48, 49, 58, 64 background; State Archives, Cape Town 11, 14; South African Library, Cape Town 12; Topham Picturepoint 15 (Associated; Press), 31 and 34 background (Keystone); Hulton Getty Picture Collection 18t, 43b (Keystone), *Journal of South African History*, No. 36, 1955, CUP 16; *Die Burgher* 17; *The Cape Times* 20t and b, 23, 30t, 31b, 50; George Hallett 25t; Jurgen Schadeburg 25b, 26b, 37, 39b, 43tl; Bailey's African History Archives 29, 32, 39t, 45; Abe Berry, *Act by Act* 33; Orde Eliason/Link Picture Library 46, 56t, 58t, Greg English/Link Picture Library 57b, 59, 60; *Rand Daily Mail* 47; Frank Spooner Pictures 51 background; *Images of Defiance*, South African History Archive 56b, 57t; Walter Dhladhla/Link 61t and 61b; Popperfotto 62b, 63 (Reuter/Dufka), 64 inset (Reuter/Andrews); Corbis-Bettman 62t (Reuter/Andrews)

# Contents

# Apartheid – old wine in new bottles?

In 1948, the Purified National Party came to power in South Africa. Its aim was to turn South Africa into a republic and to separate the various racial groups within the country.

## Why did many white South Africans support republican, racist ideas in 1948?

In 1948, Daniel Francois Malan, a minister of the Dutch Reformed Church, became Prime Minister of South Africa. In the election campaign, he promised those who voted for him that he would make South Africa a republic and an apartheid state. Why did these promises bring him victory? Had white South Africans always been racist? Were racist policies exclusive to Afrikaners? Why was republicanism so appealing?

### Racism

The origins of racism and its appeal lie deep in South Africa's history. The first European colonists, the Dutch, settled at the Cape of Good Hope in 1652 with the intention of establishing a base from which they could supply their East Indies Fleet. Other Europeans, mainly German and some French, also made their home in the Cape. The settlers came in contact with the indigenous people of the area – the Khoisan, a people made up of two groups – the Khoikhoi whom the settlers called the 'Hottentots' and the San known as 'Bushmen'. In the beginning, there was much co-operation between the new settlers and the indigenous people. But, when some Dutch East India Company employees became farmers, they wanted more and more land. As a result, serious conflict with the Khoi pastoralists and hunter-gatherers began. Because slaves were brought in from the East Indies, menial work soon became associated with people of colour and this affected the attitudes of some settlers. Eventually many Khoikhoi became servants and the San were persecuted and often killed.

As the Dutch began to expand eastward, they came in contact with the Xhosa people. These were mainly settled farmers and better able to defend their territory than the Khoikhoi. Sometimes they co-operated with the Dutch or made an uneasy truce with them but often their relationship became hostile. War broke out for the first time between the settlers and the Xhosa in 1779.

**SOURCE A**

*A coloured lithograph of around 1836 showing Boers hunting down Khoisan accused of stealing cattle.*

The British, who wanted to protect their sea route to India, took the Cape from the Dutch in 1806. In 1828, they abolished the Hottentot Codes, strict regulations – including the carrying of passes – that had been introduced by the British Governor, Lord Caledon, in 1809. In 1833, the British abolished slavery.

## The origins of republicanism

The seeds of republicanism were sown in 1836 when a large number of Afrikaner farmers, known as the 'Voortrekkers', moved northwards into the interior in search of land. They wished to get away from a war-torn eastern Cape, the rule of the British, and to be free to speak their own language and control their own affairs. The journey later became known as the Great Trek. This event, and the subsequent battles they had with some of the black kingdoms in the interior, were used many years later by some Afrikaner leaders to build a sense of Afrikaner identity.

The British passed laws that attempted to gain control over the Voortrekkers beyond the bounds of the Cape Colony. In 1842, the British took over Port Natal (Durban). This was resented by the Voortrekkers, many of whom again moved into the interior. By 1850, the colonial office had decided that any attempt to control the lands beyond the Cape Colony and Natal was a profitless and expensive task. They signed treaties granting the Boers the lands beyond the Orange and Vaal Rivers in 1852 and 1854, so the Orange Free State and the South African Republic (Transvaal) came into being.

### AFRIKANERS

Afrikaners are people of European descent, usually Dutch, German or French, who made their home in Africa. At first they spoke Dutch but the language gradually changed. Local African words were adopted and it became a new language called Afrikaans. The Afrikaners are also called Boers, which means farmers. The first Afrikaans newspaper, *Die Afrikaanse Patriot*, was published in January 1876. It stood for 'our language, our nation and our country'. The founding of the newspaper highlights the growing tradition of nationalism among the Boers that Malan, the leader of the Purified National Party, was able to draw on in 1948.

**SOURCE B**

*An illustration of 1849 showing Utimi, the nephew of the Zulu warrior hero and chief Shaka Zulu. As the Boers moved into KwaZulu (Natal), the Zulu defended their territory.*

## Federation

The two Boer Republics were mostly left alone by the British until, in the late 1860s, diamonds and gold were discovered inside their borders.

The British government was anxious to control the huge potential profits from the new-found diamonds and gold. They were also concerned that the Boers might be encouraged by these huge profits to demand formal independence and to assert Boer sovereignty. Lord Carnarvon, the British Secretary of State for Colonies from 1874 to 1878, hoped that, if the four republics could be joined together in a federation (or political union), these problems could be solved. The British also felt that a federation of four states would be able to stand up to outside interference from other European powers, like Germany, who wanted to extend their influence in Africa.

The British, therefore, took steps to bring about federation in a number of ways. Firstly, the Afrikaner diamond-fields were incorporated into the Cape Colony in 1871. Secondly, the South African Republic (Transvaal) was annexed in 1877. Finally, from 1877 to 1879, the British fought a series of wars against the independent black kingdoms of South Africa, like Zululand and Lesotho, in order to gain control over them.

## SOURCE C

## The Anglo-Boer Wars

The Boer Republics fought twice for their survival against Britain, once in 1880–81 and again from 1899 to 1902. By the end of the second war, most Afrikaners had come to despise the British administration and the way in which the wars had been conducted. The scorched-earth policy ordered by the leader of the British forces, General Kitchener, that had destroyed their farms, and the deaths of 25,000 women and children in concentration camps had left them bitter and resentful.

## SOUTH AFRICA AT THE TIME OF THE 1899–1902 WAR

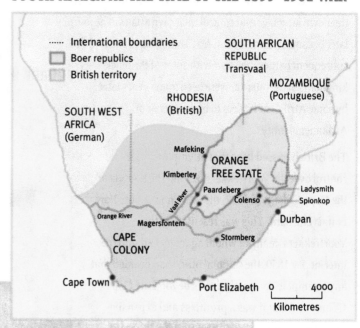

A typical Boer commando unit made up of farmers and townspeople. Raiding parties such as these successfully harassed the British lines of communications during the war of 1899–1902. They were excellent marksmen.

## SOURCE D

*One of the concentration camps established for Boers during the war. Many people, especially children, died from disease and starvation. Thousands of black people were put into separate concentration camps during the Boer war. At least 14,000 of them died because of this treatment.*

## SOURCE E

*When families returned from the camps they often found their farms had been totally destroyed. One farmer remembers the scene that met him on returning to his farm:*

We had nothing – no furniture, no cooking facilities. We didn't have a stove and if we had had a stove we had nothing to put on the stove not in the way of either utensils or food. And they killed everything, every chicken and every pig and every sheep – every animal on the farm. There was nothing on the farm. Nothing on any farm.

Quoted in David Harrison, *The White Tribe of Africa*, 1981

After the war, Lord Alfred Milner, the British High Commissioner in South Africa, adopted a policy of 'Anglicisation'. He was anxious to break down the sharp divisions between the Boers and the mainly town-dwelling British. He wanted to encourage large numbers of new British settlers to come to South Africa, hoping that they would swamp the Boers. But this simply did not happen. Milner also insisted that English should be the only means of instruction in all schools. This policy, which was not supported by all his colleagues, was bitterly resented by the Boers as they felt that the Boer language and culture was being threatened. These feelings of resentment helped to keep republicanism alive among the Boers.

## Segregation

After the 1905 General Election in Britain, the new Liberal government decided that it would be in Britain's best interests to co-operate with the Afrikaner communities in South Africa. The Liberals had been opposed to the use of force in the Anglo-Boer War and were ashamed of the use of concentration camps and the wholesale destruction of the Boer farms. They also knew that, as the Afrikaners were in a majority, they would dominate any future government. The British, therefore, tried to placate the Afrikaners to a certain extent during negotiations leading to the creation of the Union of South Africa in 1910. As a result, the practices by which the races had been segregated in the two Boer republics now became part of the new Constitution. A commission, the South African Native Affairs Commission, that had been set up by the British politician, Lord Milner, reported in 1905. It proposed segregation as the right policy for the country. This policy was to be carried out and further extended by governments after 1910.

## >> Activity

Explain in your own words how:

**a** European people came into conflict with black people;

**b** Afrikaners became hostile to the British government.

# Legislation for inequality 1910–48

Between the years 1910 and 1948 the policy of separating the various racial groups in South Africa was enacted in law. Segregation eventually began to break down only when it became a handicap to economic growth.

## The Union of South Africa

In 1910, the British colonies (the Cape Colony and Natal) and the former Boer republics – the Orange Free State and the South African Republic (Transvaal) – were joined in a political union. The negotiations had, on the whole, pleased the Afrikaners. In future elections, for example, the voting arrangements laid down in the Constitution would give greater weight to votes cast in the rural areas. This meant that the Afrikaners (who were mainly farmers) could be sure of having political control. Each member state, moreover, was allowed to keep the voting system that had existed before the union. This meant that blacks and coloureds had only a qualified right (based on the ownership of property) to vote in the Cape and no vote at all in the Orange Free State, Transvaal or Natal.

## RACIAL GROUPS IN SOUTH AFRICA

*African*
These were the original black inhabitants of South Africa. Various words were used to describe them such as Natives, Non-Europeans, Bantu, or Africans.

*White*
These were made up of the Afrikaans speakers, mainly of Dutch, German and French descent, and the English-speaking colonists, mainly of British descent, who were in the minority.

*Coloured*
The Coloured community is a mixture of the various population groups of South Africa. Many are descended from the skilled Batavian slaves (from present-day Java) brought to South Africa by the Dutch. The ancestors of others were whites, free blacks, Khoisan, and slaves from Madagascar and east and west Africa.

*Asian*
The Asian community was largely descended from Indian immigrants. Many of these had been brought over in the nineteenth century to work on the sugar plantations of Natal. Some higher-caste Indians had also come over at their own expense to work in Natal, mainly as traders.

In 1914, a delegation of the South African Native National Congress came to London to try (unsuccessfully) to gain the support of the British government against the colour bar in South Africa.

## Black protest

The black, Coloured and Indian communities were dismayed to see the colour bar enshrined in the new legislation. The first national association for black people, the South African Native National Congress (SANNC), was founded in 1912. In 1923, it was to change its name to the African National Congress (ANC). Most of its members were lawyers, teachers or priests from the newly emerging black middle classes. Their protests were vigorous but peaceful. But the two South African prime ministers who were largely to dominate political life before 1948, J. C. Smuts and B. M. Hertzog, were convinced segregationists and all protest fell on deaf ears.

## Discrimination

In the years that followed, successive governments passed Acts extending discrimination on the grounds of race in many areas where it had not existed before, until it covered nearly all aspects of daily life.

The attitudes behind these Acts of Parliament were summed up by the Stallard Commission of 1922 when it stated that 'blacks were in towns to minister to the needs of the white man and should depart when they cease to minister'.

### ACTS DISCRIMINATING ON GROUNDS OF RACE

**1911:** Blacks were barred from many categories of work.

**1913:** The Native Land Act forbade blacks to own land (except in a few native reserves making up 7.3 per cent of the total land) and forbade them to practise share-cropping. This was a practice whereby tenants farmed the land and gave back a proportion of the crops to the landlord as a form of rent.

**1923:** The Urban Areas Act created special areas, well away from city centres, where black people could be forced to live.

**1924:** Certain unskilled jobs were reserved only for whites.

**1924:** The Industrial Conciliation Act forbade any 'pass bearer' (that is, blacks) from taking part in trade-union activity.

**1926:** The Colour Bar Act prevented blacks and Asians from doing skilled and semi-skilled jobs in mines.

**1927:** An Immorality Act forbade extra-marital sex between whites and blacks.

**1936:** Another Land Act severely limited the rights of black people to lease property, operate businesses or own agricultural land.

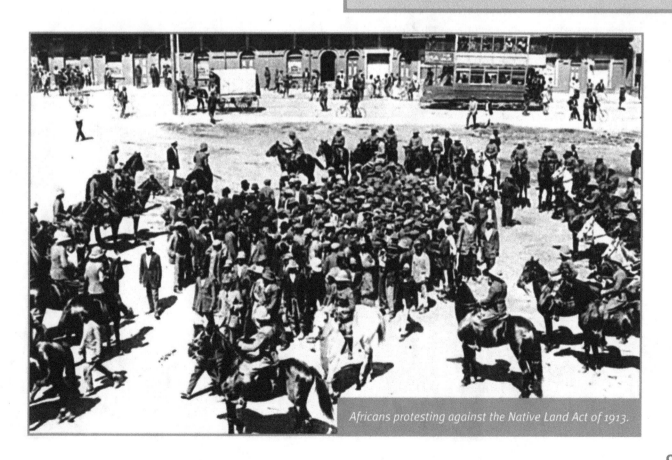

*Africans protesting against the Native Land Act of 1913.*

## REASONS FOR THE GOVERNMENT'S SEGREGATION POLICY

Historians have suggested a number of reasons as to why successive governments adopted policies of segregation.

1  It kept blacks in an inferior position and enabled employers to pay them low wages.

2  It gave white workers protection against competition.

3  It limited the black people's control over land and thus freed it for white farmers.

4  There was a great deal of industrial unrest in South Africa in the first quarter of the twentieth century. Employers and political leaders feared what would happen if all workers joined together in opposing them. They tried to control the workforce by creating divisions between black and white.

5  Many people in nineteenth-century Europe and America had believed that the white race was superior to all others. These white supremacist views were readily adopted in the new Union of South Africa.

6  Some people thought that the native African should be encouraged to live in 'natural conditions' away from the corrupting effects of towns and industry. Others felt that segregation and the creation of native reserves would preserve tribal unity and purity and that it was important to keep African people separate in order to protect their culture.

## PASSES

Before 1828, blacks in the Cape had had to carry passes in order to work on white farms. In that year the practice had been abolished but, gradually, passes for black workers came back into use. By 1910, blacks needed to possess a number of different documents, such as travel passes, work passes, residential passes or curfew passes. If they failed to produce them when challenged by officials they were punished. These Pass Laws were bitterly resented.

## Discussion points

> How did the government discriminate against black people?

> Look at the list of reasons given for the policy of segregation. How many are to do with economics?

An African pass book. Passes were used in South Africa, as they were in Russia, to stop the free movement of the people from rural to urban areas. They gave the authorities a powerful method of control.

# Politics in a changing society

Hardline attitudes developed during the early decades of the twentieth century.
Many internal and external factors encouraged the spread of segregationist ideas.

## Why did support for segregationist policies increase within South Africa from 1910 to 1938?

After 1910 many people moved into towns and industry was growing rapidly. Certain other events that took place in the 1930s, however, were equally important in influencing the new state to pass segregationist laws. The most important of these events were the Great Depression, the spread of fascist ideas, and the Second World War of 1939 to 1945. All these influenced politics within South Africa.

### Resentment among white workers

Governments were well aware how important gold and diamonds were for the economy and they tended to favour the interests of the powerful mining houses. Labour was provided by black men who migrated from their villages to the mines and worked on short contracts. They were housed together in male-only compounds. This system suited the mining companies who were able to supervise their workers and keep the black workers segregated from the whites.

In the early years of the twentieth century, the gold-mining industry had gone through a period of stagnation. The mining companies, therefore, attempted to cut costs by raising the ratio of black to white workers. They also considered whether they should employ a proportion of settled black labour rather than migratory black labour in the mines. Another way of cutting costs was to employ black workers for the skilled work which had previously been reserved for whites. The white workers responded to this threat in 1913 and again in 1922 with strikes. The strikes were firmly crushed, but the politicians had had a glimpse of just how powerful the workers could be. The Prime Minister at the time, General J. C. Smuts, of the South African Party, became unpopular with many white workers as he came to be regarded as an ally of big business.

In the election of 1924, a coalition government of the Labour Party and Nationalist Party won power. The Nationalist Party had been founded by General B. M. Hertzog in 1914 to protect and promote Afrikaner national interests. This new government combined white workers' support for the Labour Party in the towns and Afrikaner support in the rural areas. It was also committed to further racial segregation.

SOURCE A

*Black mine workers in the De Beers compound.*

**SOURCE B**

*The home of a poor white family, from the Carnegie Commission Report of 1932.*

## The problem of 'poor whites'

After the ending of the Anglo-Boer War many Boer farmers had suffered from the effects of the wholesale burning of their farms. Poverty amongst the farmers was made worse first by an outbreak of rinderpest among cattle at the end of the nineteenth century and then a severe drought from 1907 to 1908. During the 1920s and 1930s, as the price of land rose, landlords bought up large tracts of land, driving off many of the tenant farmers and hiring labourers in their place.

In 1932, the Carnegie Commission was set up to examine the extent of poverty amongst whites. It found that over 20 per cent of Afrikaner males had no means of providing a livelihood for themselves and their wives and children. South Africa had to acknowledge that it had a 'poor-white' problem.

## The politicians' response to white grievances

Politicians began to compete with one another to win the support of these disgruntled sections of society. White workers were important to politicians for two reasons. Firstly, they had the vote and could make or break a political party. Secondly, if white trade union leaders allowed black workers into their organisations, the unions would be in a powerful position to demand an improvement in their terms and conditions of employment. Those in powerful positions began to feel that it was vital to prevent workers of different races from uniting. They also realised that they had to solve the poor-white problem as quickly as possible.

In the 1920s, the government tried to pacify the white workers by reducing unemployment. It established state corporations, such as the Iron and Steel Corporation (ISCOR) and the Electricity Supply Commission (ESCOM). These companies, together with the state-owned railways, were used to absorb many unemployed whites. Many of these jobs were created for them at the expense of blacks.

At the same time, the rights of black tenant farmers and share-croppers were further reduced, and many were forced to become wage-labourers on farms. Others moved to the cities where they competed for jobs with the unemployed white workers.

## Changes to the voting system

As the Act of Union in 1910 had formalised the voting rights already existing in the four republics, all white males had been given the vote. In 1930, white women over 21 were given the vote, largely to dilute the small black vote and make it ineffective. In 1936, the black voters in the Cape had their voting rights taken from them. In future they could only elect three white representatives under a separate system.

## The creation of the United Party

The effects of the Great Depression in the early 1930s meant that times remained hard for the workers. These difficult years brought about a coalition of the two major political parties. The Nationalist Party under General B. M. Hertzog joined forces with the opposition South African Party, now led by General Jan Smuts. This coalition, known as the United Party, governed South Africa from 1933.

## Trade unions and the Labour Party gain support

During 1933, the international price of gold went up by 45 per cent and continued to climb. The state received £4.3 million in 1932 in taxes. In 1933, it collected £14.5 million. The workers, both black and white, however, did not benefit from this bonanza. Their real wages, in fact, dropped from 1936 onward. The state used its income to assist white landowners and manufacturing industry. But the economic boom brought about by the rising price of gold made more jobs available. Afrikaner women found regular employment in factories, and began to assert their independence. Many Afrikaners joined trade unions and swelled the support of the country's small Labour Party.

## The Purified National Party

Afrikaner leaders were afraid that their traditional hold over the Afrikaner population would weaken as a result of these economic and social changes. They, therefore, tried to unite Afrikaners of all classes behind them by encouraging strong nationalist feelings. They put forward a policy of white supremacy and spoke of a vision of the Afrikaner people united in their mission to uphold white Christian civilisation in South Africa. They were supported both by the Dutch Reformed Church and by the Broederbond. This was a secretive, but very powerful, society of white Afrikaner males. Its influence extended into every area of public life. Members were anxious to promote Afrikaner nationalism, and to advance Afrikaners in business and the professions.

In 1934, Dr D. F. Malan, a minister of the Dutch Reformed Church, broke away from Hertzog's Nationalists and founded a new party to promote these ideas. The Purified National Party, as it was first called, catered both for those who believed in white supremacy and for those who wanted South Africa to become a republic. It also appealed to those who were anxious for some kind of security in a world which was changing. Dr Malan stressed the 'sin' of racial mixing and proposed a solution – apartheid.

### APARTHEID

The word apartheid originated in the 1930s amongst Afrikaner intellectuals. They were strongly influenced by fascist ideas which had become popular in Germany, Italy and Spain. They argued for a complete vertical separation between all racial groups, with blacks only coming into towns to work.

In 1948, the National Party were to appoint a Committee under P. O. Sauer to draft an apartheid policy that would appeal to the voters. Dr H. F. Verwoerd, Prime Minister from 1958 to 1961, would later be responsible for turning apartheid into a doctrine.

## BLOOD RIVER

On 16 December 1838, 500 Boers fought the Zulu Army at Blood River and won. In doing so, they avenged the death of their leader, Piet Retief and his companions who had been killed by order of Dingaan, the Zulu king. Both events became legendary and were commemorated by nationalists on the Day of the Vow (16 December) when they thanked God for their victory.

## SOURCE C

*From the late 1930s the Afrikaner leaders set about creating a strong nationalist identity. On 16 December 1938, on the 100th anniversary of the victory at Blood River, the steps of the Voortrekkers were traced in a pilgrimage across South Africa, with gatherings attended by huge crowds.*

*Dr Malan gave the main address at Blood River. He said that in 1838, by God's Grace and self-sacrifice of the Voortrekkers, Afrikanerdom had prevailed. Now, he said, Afrikaners faced a new Blood River:*

In that new Blood River, black and white meet together in much closer contact and in a much more binding struggle. Today black and white jostle together in the same labour market. Their [the Voortrekkers'] freedom was also and above all the freedom to preserve themselves as a White race. You realise today [that] their task to make South Africa a white man's land is ten times more your task. As a sign of your national pride you are naming your streets after Voortrekker heroes and demanding that *Die Stem van Suid-Afrika* should be recognised as your national anthem. Have you the patriotism and sufficient power, in this year of celebration, to use this God-given opportunity also to demand something infinitely more important: the assurance that White Civilisation will be assured?

## SOURCE D

*A later illustration of the victory at Blood River on 16 December 1838.*

## SOURCE E

*Hester Cornelius, an Afrikaner woman, describes how she became a trade unionist:*

In 1930, at the age of twenty-two, I came to Johannesburg to look for work. There were hundreds of girls looking for jobs. I returned to the farm and became an ardent Nationalist, believing that the South African Party was to blame for our poverty and unemployment. Later, I returned to Johannesburg and found work.

I began to fight for my rights and the rights of my fellow-workers almost immediately I started work in a factory. Then I heard about the Garment Workers' Union. The more I saw of the union activities, the more I realised how necessary it was for the workers to become organised.

At first I could not understand why Mr Sachs [secretary of the union], who was a Jew, fought so hard for the Afrikaner daughters. I spoke to many Nationalists. They attacked him bitterly and this made me lose faith in the Nationalist Party. [I understood that] if the workers were organised and united, they could gain higher wages and a better life.

The first strike in which I took a leading part was in 1936, in Cape Town ... I was arrested.

Over twenty years have passed since I started work in the clothing industry and, during that period, there has been a complete change in our wages, conditions of work and way of life. It was the union which set us free from the hell of starvation wages. The Nationalists have never helped us. On the contrary, they have always tried to break our union.

## SOURCE F

**Solly Sachs was later banned by the government and arrested in 1950 while he was addressing a meeting of the union in Johannesburg. Here the crowd rush towards the police who are holding Mr Sachs on the left of the picture.**

## SOURCE G

*The reply the organisers of the 1938 Centenary Trek sent to Solly Sachs when he asked if some of his union members, most of whom were Afrikaner women, could take part in the celebrations in Pretoria, shows clearly why many feared the growth of unions:*

The Afrikaner nation is busy united to mobilise its forces against you and your sort. The thousands of Afrikaner daughters whom you have in your clutches will settle with you .... Our people do not want anything to do with Communists and Jews .... You and Johanna Cornelius [a union official] who all day long organise and address Kaffirs [an insulting reference to blacks], will you dare to bring them also to the celebrations?

SOURCE H

Dr Malan's poster prepared for the 1938 election. The woman in the poster is
'The hope of South Africa' and she urges readers to 'vote for the National Party and
protect my people and my posterity'. The smaller pictures reveal the 'dangers' to
which she is subjected. On the left the caption reads 'Mixed Marriages which the
United Party will not prohibit by Law'. In the right-hand picture the caption reads
'Fusion with foreign elements' and the sinister figures represent the capitalist,
the communist, the imperialist and the Jew.

>> Activity

1 Why were many poor
   white people resentful
   in the 1920s?

2 Why do you think some
   people celebrated Blood
   River?

3 How did the Nationalists
   view the trade union
   movement?

4 Look at Source H.

   a What prejudices
      does it reveal?

   b What fears does it
      play upon?

   c Which party in Europe
      in the 1930s might have
      used such a poster?

# The impact of the Second World War

The Second World War (1939–45) brought changes to South Africa which worried many white people.

## Why were many whites threatened by the changes which took place during the war?

The decision to join the Allies in the war had split the United Party. Both its leading politicians, Hertzog and Smuts, were Boer generals who had fought against the British in the war of 1899–1902. At the time of Union they adopted different attitudes. Smuts believed that South Africa's best interests lay in co-operation with Britain. Hertzog had founded the first Afrikaner Nationalist Party partly in protest against South Africa joining Britain in the First World War. When the Second World War broke out in 1939, South Africa was again faced with the same decision. Hertzog, who was then Prime Minister, would not agree to fight a war on the side of Britain. He was outvoted and resigned from politics. Smuts became Prime Minister and leader of the United Party.

### Segregation questioned

During the war years, South Africa was cut off from its usual suppliers of manufactured goods. As a result the economy expanded and new industries were established within South Africa. With 186,000 white men in the army, black workers were in demand. A wave of migration to the cities created a shortage of accommodation. The new industries began to take over from mining as the major employer of labour. Many industrialists began to realise that there were many disadvantages in employing migrant labour. They began to believe that it would be better to allow black workers to settle near their place of work. This would mean granting black people the right to live in the cities. In 1942, pass-law enforcement was relaxed. A Health Commission (1944) recommended a non-racial health-care programme. Liberal members of the government suggested that segregation be dropped.

**SOURCE A**

*A cartoon from* Die Burger, *in 1943, showing the Afrikaner view of Smuts as a tool of British imperialism.*

## SOURCE B

*Clashes between the police and black mine workers during the 1946 strike in Johannesburg.*

### Strikes among black workers

Increased job opportunities and good intentions did not mean good wages or housing. The black workers were frustrated at the bad conditions in which they lived and at their low wages. Many joined a union, and began to organise protests such as rent boycotts, bus boycotts, strikes, stayaways and anti-pass protests. There was a dramatic increase in the number of strikes and man-days lost between 1940 and 1945.

As the blacks had only meagre wages to support them, as many as 90,000 people were forced to settle in squatter camps in or near Johannesburg in the 1940s. These wartime developments alarmed many white people, and would later make them more willing to support Malan's Purified National Party.

## SOURCE C

*A black squatter settlement near Johannesburg in the 1940s.*

---

### INDUSTRIAL UNREST DURING THE WAR YEARS

'Twenty-five Native Strikes in Six Months', *Rand Daily Mail*, 30 January 1943

| Year | Strikes | Whites | Blacks | Man-days lost |
|------|---------|--------|--------|---------------|
| 1940 | 24 | 1200 | 700 | 6500 |
| 1941 | 35 | 700 | 4800 | 23200 |
| 1942 | 58 | 1300 | 12800 | 49500 |
| 1943 | 52 | 1800 | 7400 | 47700 |
| 1944 | 52 | 200 | 12000 | 62700 |
| 1945 | 63 | 1500 | 14700 | 91100 |

L. Callinicos, *A Place in the City*, 1993

---

### AVERAGE WAGES FOR BLACK WORKERS, 1942–3

| Sector | Wage |
|--------|------|
| Water supply | 12/6 (62$\frac{1}{2}$p) |
| Power | 12/6 (62$\frac{1}{2}$p) |
| Mining | 16/- to 20/- (80p – £1.00) |
| Timber | 16/- to 20/- (80p – £1.00) |
| Iron and steel | 21/- per week (unskilled) (£1.05) |
| | 24/- per week (semi-skilled) (£1.20) |

The lowest possible living standards required earnings of 37/6 a week (£1.87$\frac{1}{2}$).

L. Callinicos, *A Place in the City*, 1993

---

## >> Activity

1 List all the important changes which took place in South Africa during the Second World War. For each change, explain why it may have been resented by some white people.

# 1948 – Triumph of the Nationalists

## A minority wins

In 1948, whites returning from the war found it difficult to obtain work. Farmers needed labourers but many of the former rural workers had moved to the towns. Food prices were held down by the government to calm unrest in the cities, but this did not suit the farmers. Afrikaners thought that Smuts was much too involved in international affairs, and too closely allied with Britain. National Socialist ideas, developed by Hitler, with their emphasis on racial purity, had been defeated in the Second World War. They still had influence, however, on Afrikaner thinking. Before the war a number of Afrikaner politicians and academics had either visited Germany or studied there. They had approved of its political philosophy and adapted some of its ideas to suit that section of the population that felt threatened by developments in South Africa. These and other negative factors swung the 1948 general election in Malan's favour by a small but significant fraction.

## Why the National Party won the election

In the election the United Party and the Labour Party between them won 53 per cent of the votes while Malan's apartheid National Party only gained 39 per cent. The National Party won the election because of the clause in the Constitution of 1910 that had given rural areas a larger weighting. This allowed Malan to win the greater number of parliamentary seats as much of his support came from the countryside.

His party had conducted a very efficient election campaign. It had relied on such organisations as the Broederbond and the Federation of Afrikaner Cultural Associations to promote its policies. It also had the support of the *Nasionale Pers* (the National Press), which controlled a number of publications.

Strong emotions were aroused among Afrikaners by cultural festivals such as the 1938 centenary celebration of the Great Trek. Party leaders were able to use these feelings to their own advantage. Trade unions were portrayed as a 'foreign' (British) import at variance with Afrikanerdom. Afrikaner banks and businessmen were encouraged to provide capital to assist small businesses and this increased support for the party. Malan played upon the fear and greed of the voters to win support for his policies.

Many factors influenced the voters in 1948, but one of the most important was the uncertainty people felt because of the rapid changes taking place in society. Malan's policy was not fully worked out in detail before the election, but its broad outline appealed to what those who felt threatened saw as their own best interests. In 1947, King George VI and his family visited South Africa. This seemed to stress the British sympathies of General Smuts and his party. The Nationalists, with their hard-hitting campaign, won over the Transvaal farmers and the white workers of the Witwatersrand   the industrial heart of South Africa.

The new Prime Minister, Dr Malan, with his wife and two sons at home.

### The consequences of Malan's victory

The rule of the Nationalists was thought by many at that time to be only a temporary lapse. It would, in fact, last almost fifty years and devastate millions of lives. It meant that, just as the rest of the world was moving towards greater understanding and tolerance between races, the racial groups in South Africa would be more deeply separated than ever. As early as October 1949 Smuts warned South Africa of possible future isolation.

## GRAVE WARNING ISSUED BY GEN. SMUTS

### Consequences of Rule by Nationalists

## MENACE OF POLICY OF ISOLATION

The Argus Correspondent

**Maritzburg Wednesday**

SOUTH AFRICA must stand for the democratic outlook which united it with the West and cut adrift from the isolationist policies of the Nationalist Government if South Africans were to be respected among the nations of the world, said General Smuts when he opened the Natal Provincial Congress of the United Party in Maritzburg today.

General Smuts said he could not conceive anything more likely to disrupt South Africa than the pressing of a republican policy on the people.

The *Cape Argus*, 12 October 1949

A cartoon from the Cape Times, of 18 November 1948.
> What does this cartoon say about the campaign?

## Discussion points

> Why did Malan come to power in 1948? What do you think was the most important reason?

> Why was Smuts concerned by the victory of the Nationalists?

Supporters greet General Smuts after his defeat in 1948. A photograph from the Cape Times, of 9 July 1948.

# The making of the apartheid state

## Segregation

Segregation had been part of the slave-owning Cape Colony's practice since earliest times and, after the second Boer War, was formalised by the British administrators. The new Union of South Africa legalised many aspects of segregation and many laws were passed between 1911 and 1936 which discriminated on the grounds of race. During the Second World War, however, segregation started to break down.

## THE ROOTS OF REPUBLICANISM

> The Afrikaners tried to escape British jurisdiction in 1838, when they journeyed into the interior. In 1852 and 1854, the British recognised the Boer republics which had been established beyond the Orange and Vaal Rivers.

> Britain annexed the diamond-fields in 1871 and the Transvaal Republic in 1877.

> Britain fought the Boers twice for control of their republics, first from 1880 to 1881, and then from 1899 to 1902.

> The second war ended in a scorched-earth destruction of Boer farms and, during the war, thousands of women and children died in the British concentration camps.

> After the war, Lord Milner adopted a policy of Anglicisation that threatened Boer language and culture.

> Afrikaners saw themselves as having built their nation through a series of conflicts with the British, on the one hand, and the armies of the African kingdoms on the other.

## INDUSTRIALISATION AND ITS CONSEQUENCES

> Mineral discoveries started a process of industrialisation and urbanisation in South Africa.

> Politicians saw the advantage of gaining the support of the white working class.

> The Second World War forced the development of secondary industry by cutting South Africa off from traditional suppliers.

> The towns grew rapidly and segregation began to break down as the need for workers increased.

> Strikes and general labour unrest occurred from 1940 to 1945.

> The rapid growth of towns created slum conditions in major cities. The last arrivals to the urban workforce, the black people, were generally the ones living in the worst conditions.

> Soldiers returning from the war found it difficult to secure employment.

## The rise of the Nationalists

After the Second World War, the National Party came to power under Dr Malan. Their policies meant that racial groups became increasingly divided and they were to remain in power for nearly 50 years.

# The apartheid state

Dr Malan's party was elected on a programme of apartheid. But few voters fully understood what that meant. It was a policy that had not yet fully evolved.

## Legalising the apartheid state

After the election. Dr Malan immediately pushed a number of Acts through Parliament that discriminated against blacks, Coloureds and Indians. They were designed to separate the various racial groups in South Africa.

### RACIAL GROUPS IN SOUTH AFRICA AT THE TIME OF THE 1946 CENSUS

Total population 11,415,945

69 per cent African

21 per cent White

8 per cent Coloured

2 per cent Asian

### IMPORTANT ACTS OF PARLIAMENT IN THE 1950S

1949 Prohibition of Mixed Marriages

1950 Immorality Act

1950 *The Population Registration Act* meant that everyone born in South Africa was classified according to race. Bizarre methods were sometimes used that could result in members of the same family being classified into different 'racial' groups.

1950 *The Group Areas Act* set aside special residential and business areas for the different groups. This Act was most often used to remove Coloured and Indian businessmen and their families from suburbs which, later, would be made available to poor whites.

1950 *The Suppression of Communism Act* made the Communist Party and any other related organisation illegal. The Act was drafted in such a way that it could be used to prevent people from exercising their civil rights and demonstrating for any kind of political, industrial, social or economic change.

1951 *The Bantu Authorities Act* granted local self-government to particular areas, usually under government-approved chiefs.

1952 *The Native Laws Amendment Act* said that blacks could only live permanently in an urban area if they had been born there or had lived there continuously for 15 years, or had worked there for the same employer continuously for 10 years.

1952 *The Abolition of Passes Act* withdrew the documents that controlled the movement of blacks but replaced them with a detailed 96-page reference book which also contained the holder's fingerprints.

1953 Bantu Education Act

1953 *The Criminal Law Amendment Act* imposed heavy fines, terms of imprisonment, or corporal punishment for protesting against any law.

1953 *The Reservation of Separate Amenities Act* segregated all public amenities like beaches, buses, trains, right down to the park benches.

1956 Separate Representation of Voters Act

1957 State-aided Institutions Act

1957/58 Job Reservation Acts

1959 *The Extension of Universities Act*, rather than 'extending' universities, limited admission to the established universities to whites. It provided for the creation of new universities that were to be sited in the homelands. They later came to be known as 'tribal' colleges.

These Acts forced people to live in separate areas, use separate schools, transport and other public facilities. The Prohibition of Mixed Marriages Act forbade inter-racial marriage and the Immorality Act made sex between people from different racial groups illegal. Black men were forced to register and carry pass-books with them at all times. Everybody was 'classified' according to race. Selected jobs were reserved for whites. An inferior school curriculum was drawn up for blacks. It would ensure that, in future years, they would pose little threat to white workers. The architects of the apartheid system justified their laws by promising all blacks full rights in their own areas. Special areas, shown on the map on page 27, were set aside for blacks. Every black person had to be attached, as a citizen, to one of these areas, which were to become known as Bantustans (homelands). It was intended that their language and culture would be protected in these areas where, eventually, they would be given full political control. The Bantustans were supposedly the areas in which various clans had lived prior to white settlement. Each area was given self-government and later some were given 'independence'.

## Discussion point

> What sort of changes were brought in by the new government?

*A cartoon from the* Cape Times, *of 17 June 1950. This cartoon shows the new repressive laws killing freedom and civil liberties in South Africa.*

# Apartheid in practice

Separate areas where people of a particular racial or religious group were concentrated, like ghettos, had often existed in countries around the world, but never before had the separation of different racial groups been imposed by force on such a massive scale.

## What did separation mean in South Africa after 1948?

### Physical segregation – the towns

In order to enforce apartheid, all the various racial groups had to be physically separated from each other. The areas where people of different racial groups could live had to be strictly controlled. In this way one of the strangest attempts at social engineering in history began.

*The Group Areas Act*
In 1956, five group areas had been set up by the Act. These were areas 'designated' for particular racial groups. By 1987, there were more than 1,300. A complex administrative system was set up by which land was confiscated from some groups and allocated to

**SOURCE A**

### Malan Announces Bill to "Eliminate Mixed Residential Areas"

To eliminate mixed residential areas the Group Reservation Bill will be introduced in Parliament this session, the Prime Minister, Dr Malan, told a meeting of his constituents here tonight.

It would reserve areas for Europeans where no non-European would be allowed to own or occupy fixed property.

Areas would be reserved for Coloured people where Europeans and Natives would not be able to own or occupy fixed property.

**RESERVED FOR NATIVES**

There would also be areas reserved for Natives where Europeans and Coloureds would not be able to own or occupy fixed property.

The Bill would solve the problem of the penetration of non-Europeans into European areas.

*Rand Daily Mail,* April 1950

others, and by which people were removed from an area by force and then relocated. The system had to be run by a large body of government officials. It gave those who were corrupt many opportunities to line their own pockets.

The Group Areas Act took away the right to own property which black people had been given in some urban areas. Under the guise of 'slum-clearance' or 'town-planning' these people were relocated many miles away. Such actions sometimes made it possible for white workers, in turn, to move closer to their places of work.

It is estimated that 600,000 people – particularly those designated Coloured and Indian – were affected by this Act. In Cape Town, alone, between 1957 and 1980, 30,842 Coloured people were relocated. There was no escape, even for tenants. The legal owner of a property in a white area, for example, was not allowed to rent it to a tenant from another racial group.

**SOURCE B**

*Africans protesting at the Group Areas Act in the 1950s.*

The most famous areas cleared under the Group Areas Act were those of Sophiatown in Johannesburg, destroyed in 1955, District Six in Cape Town, where Coloured people had lived since 1838, and Cato Manor in Durban. Many other communities were broken up in similar fashion and millions of lives were ruined by the Act.

## SOURCE C

*In 1991, Amina Vallie remembered the day the Group Areas Act finally closed in on her family.*

Amina Vallie will never forget the sight of her mother closing, for the last time, the door on her Claremont home.

That image still brings tears to her eyes more than 15 years after the Group Areas Act brought to an end decades of family life in the pretty suburb below Table Mountain. 'When we went to fetch her that evening she never looked back,' says Mrs Vallie.

Now 69, Mrs Vallie had moved out of the Claremont house when she got married in 1946 and went to live in Newlands where her husband's family lived and ran a lucrative cartage business from a large property with five houses.

In the mid-1970s, having resisted for as long as they could, the Vallies were forced to sell the property to the Group Areas Board. They were paid R65,000 for the property, which the Board is reputed to have resold for R250,000.

Amina Vallie, *Leadership,* Vol. 10, 1991

## SOURCE E

*Amina Vallie, in 1991, next to the site of the house in which she used to live.*

## SOURCE D

Jurgen Schadeburg

*This defiant declaration scrawled on a Sophiatown wall was echoed in other places all over the country.*

*Sophiatown*

Any resistance was always met with force. In Sophiatown 80 trucks and 2,000 armed police moved in to relocate the people who were unwilling to move.

**SOURCE F**

*People move out with their possessions.*

**SOURCE G**

*In 1996,* The Sunday Independent *of Cape Town looked back at the consequences of the Group Areas Act:*

The non-racial suburb of Sophiatown was bulldozed and replaced by Triomf, triumph of apartheid.

But memories have never died, and many people still call the area by its old name.

Harry Danes, 54, lived in Hursthill, a nearby suburb. He watched the removals and comments, 'We saw riots and people burning homes, the army and police often had to close off the area and teach these guys a lesson.' The memory of black residents is different. They remember vividly being 'forced at gun point to get into trucks and move to Meadowlands', they also remember that we were such happy people – 'it was safe and fun being in Sophiatown'. Their homes were bulldozed. Marion Kahn states: 'I am still haunted by one question: Why did the government do this? It was the most heart-breaking experience.' This year (1996) her family will buy property in Sophiatown.

**SOURCE H**

*After the police, came the bulldozers so that no trace would be left of a once-flourishing community. The white suburb erected on the site was called Triomf (triumph).*

Jurgen Schadeburg

## Physical segregation – the countryside

The process by which land had been taken away from black people had begun with the 1913 Native Land Act. But Dr H.F. Verwoerd, as Minister of Native Affairs and, after 1958, as Prime Minister, put into operation a more complex plan that would relocate some 3.5 million people. His 1959 Bantu Self-Government Act set up eight (later ten) Bantu homelands, Bantustans, each with some degree of self-government, and extended the powers of the government-approved chiefs.

The urban forced-removals, though bitter, were carried out in full view of the public. In the rural areas, out of the public glare, millions of lives were similarly affected. The government tried to halt and reverse the flow of people to the cities. The Bantu Labour Act of 1964 made it illegal for black people to seek work in the towns. A state labour bureau was set up to administer this Act. In 1967, regulations were issued requiring black people to live in the 'homelands' when their labour was not required.

### VERWOERD

Verwoerd was born in the Netherlands in 1901 and moved to South Africa with his parents two years later. He was an extremely bright student and went on to study theology at Stellenbosch University near Cape Town. He identified with Afrikaner nationalist ideals and joined the Broederbond in the 1930s. A few years later he became editor of *Die Transvaler,* a major Afrikaans newspaper. He was a firm supporter of Malan and bitterly opposed to Smuts. In 1950, he was made Minister of Native Affairs by Malan and was the architect of the Bantu Education Act. After he became Prime Minister in 1958, he was determined to try to make apartheid acceptable to world opinion and so he developed a theory of 'separate nations' in an attempt to make apartheid respectable. He survived one attempt on his life in 1961 but was assassinated in 1966.

## THE BANTUSTANS

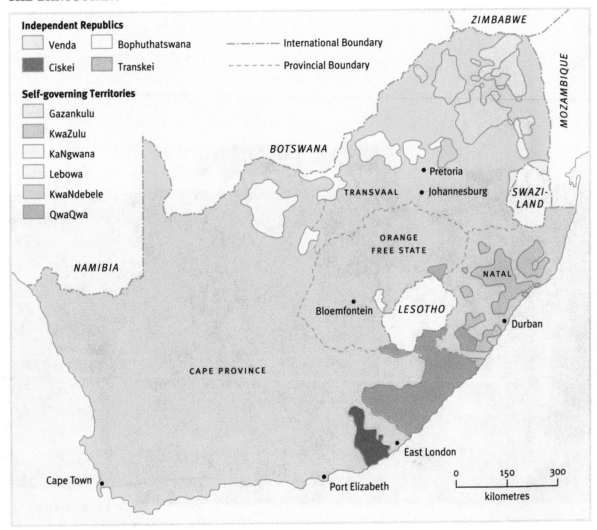

Independent Republics
- Venda
- Ciskei
- Bophuthatswana
- Transkei

International Boundary
Provincial Boundary

Self-governing Territories
- Gazankulu
- KwaZulu
- KaNgwana
- Lebowa
- KwaNdebele
- QwaQwa

## The Bantustans

In the period 1960 to 1983 the population of the Bantustans rose by 70 per cent. A committee had been set up to investigate the policy of separate development. The Tomlinson Report of 1955 had looked at the question of the homelands and claimed that they would need a large amount of central funding if the policy was to work. Verwoerd had refused to accept its findings. These areas, therefore, had no industries and amenities. They soon became overcrowded places where tribalism was promoted by the government as a means of keeping people under control. Local chiefs were used to persuade people to accept the idea of separate development. This led to the creation of an elite bureaucracy of officials who collaborated with the government and who benefited from the government's policies. Most Bantustans ultimately accepted a nominal form of 'independence'.

### SOURCE J

*A historian observed that:*

'Separate development was a bold attempt to break down a broad African nationalism and to replace it with tribal identities, led by a new class of collaborators.'

N. Worden, *The Making of Modern South Africa*, 1994

The story of Kas Maine is one which illustrates how even the resourceful were defeated by the laws of apartheid. He was born in 1894 in the Transvaal. Hard work and efficient farming methods made him a prosperous share-cropper in the years 1910 to 1957. A man of many talents, he also worked as a sheep-shearer, cobbler and mason. The apartheid state, however, caught up with him. Despite his earnings he could neither buy land nor get a bank loan. He was forced, finally, to move to Ledig in the 'homeland' of Bophuthatswana. The place was barren and unsuitable for either ploughing or grazing. There he eked out a living for the rest of his days. Apartheid impoverished an able man and denied him access to the land he had farmed successfully. He died in 1985 before apartheid was abolished.

### SOURCE I

*The resettlement area at Ledig.*

**SOURCE K**

Passes are slavery – a protest against
the inequalities of the Pass Laws.

## Passes

The laws governing the mixing of races and geographic separation
could not have been kept in being without the population register.
This classified all citizens according to race. It was supported by
the system of reference books or passes. People who did not have a
valid pass would be 'endorsed out' and sent to a homeland. Police
raided dwellings in the black townships and the servants' quarters
that were attached to many white homes to check for passes. It was
not unusual for law-abiding citizens to serve time in gaol for
'pass offences'.

## SOURCE L

*Henry Nxumalo, the editor of a magazine called* Drum, *tells us
of his experience when was arrested on a 'pass offence'. He
was out late at night without reference papers. He had never
been jailed before. Shortly after his arrest he was thrown into
a cell with 37 other prisoners. He was denied the right to
telephone friends, family or employer. He was held there for
five days.*

The reception area had a terrifying brutal atmosphere. It was
full of foul language. A number of khaki-uniformed white
officials stood behind a long cement bar-like curved counter.
When they were not joking about prisoners, they were
swearing at them and taking down their particulars. Two were

taking fingerprints and hitting the prisoners in the face when
they made mistakes.

[He, and others, were kicked, slapped and pushed around by
the warders] We were then taken to the showers in another
room. There was neither soap nor a towel. After a few minutes
under water we were told to get out and skip to get dry.

In the four days I was in prison – I got remission of one day –
I was kicked and thrashed every day. I saw many other
prisoners being thrashed daily. I was never told what was
expected of me, but had to guess. Sometimes I guessed
wrong and got into trouble.

>> **Activity**

**1** How did the government make sure that the
various racial groups were separated?

# Coloured voting rights

At the time of Union (1910), Coloured people living in Cape Colony had the right to vote. A clause in the new Constitution upheld this right. This clause could only be amended or removed by a two-thirds parliamentary majority. On taking power, Dr Malan had quickly removed the token black and Indian representation in Parliament that existed at the time (see page 13). He then set about preventing the Cape Coloured voters from voting with the whites in elections by removing them from the common roll of voters. It proved to be a difficult task.

His Bill for a limited and separate Coloured people's voters' roll went through Parliament in 1951. Immediately a group of Coloured voters challenged it in the Appeal Court. The Bill was overturned. The Prime Minister and the National Party were determined not to accept this. Malan recalled Parliament to sit as a 'High Court'. They overturned the judgment. The Coloured voters again petitioned the Appeal Court. The Appeal Court judges dismissed the action of the High Court of Parliament out of hand. The judges said that voting rights of the Coloured people could only be removed by a two-thirds vote in Parliament. Dr Malan then decided that the only way to change the law relating to Coloured voters was to create the necessary two-thirds majority in Parliament. He did this by creating six new seats to represent the South African controlled territory of South-West Africa in the House of Assembly and another four in the Senate (the Upper House).

A cartoon from the Cape Times, 17 April 1952.

## Opposition to the Bill

A non-racial movement, called the Torch Commando, was formed to demonstrate against the government's policy.

Huge protest processions were held, but the movement did not have either the strength or the organisation of a political party. The challenge brought the government unwelcome publicity but it was soon over.

In the general election of 1953, the National Party was again returned to power but without the necessary two-thirds majority. The Bill was tabled once again in Parliament, and once again defeated. The following June, Malan made another unsuccessful attempt to get the Bill passed. He retired from politics shortly afterwards with the matter unresolved.

Torch rallies call on Dr Malan to resign.

The front page of the Cape Times, 17 April 1952.

**CAPE TIMES**

UNITED FRONT FORMED TO FIGHT GOVERNMENT

Action by U.P., Labour and Torch Commando

CAMPAIGN LAUNCHED AT MASS CITY MEETING

Strauss Presents Solemn Joint Pledge

## The Separate Representation of Voters Act 1956

His successor as Prime Minister, J. G. Strijdom, was less worried about working within the Constitution. He placed new judges of his own choice in the Appeal Court and appointed additional short-term members to the Senate. The Coloured vote issue was placed before a joint sitting of Parliament and Senate. The government finally got its two-thirds majority in 1956. The carrying out of Parliament's wishes was no longer a problem. The government had packed the Civil Service with Afrikaans-speaking followers who were sympathetic to the Nationalist Party's policies.

### Discussion points

> Why do you think that Malan was keen to stop Coloured people voting?

> What evidence is there from this time that many people opposed apartheid?

# Education

## The Bantu Education Act of 1953

Education was another key area where the government sought control. In 1950, J. P. Kent, then head of the South African Teachers' Association, stated that for 'Native education' there was no turning back. Education, he said, would mean freedom and should be based on initiative and independent thought. The government, however, had a different plan.

No policy of free and compulsory education for all children had existed in South Africa. This meant that the work of missionary and community schools was even more important and they succeeded in producing some fine graduates. These schools had escaped the full weight of official interference because they often trained their own teachers. But there were too few secondary schools. The number of pupils enrolling in schools had risen 50 per cent since the war years (1939 to 1945). Private funds were in short supply. Government assistance was necessary, but its plans for the black schools were not what the parents and pupils had in mind.

The government was, in fact, already planning the most far-reaching of its repressive measures – the Bantu Education Act of 1953. The Act was introduced by Verwoerd, who was then Minister of Native Affairs. He intended to abolish the mission schools. As teachers in these schools taught liberal values and all lessons were in English they were highly valued by the community. The Act insisted that, in future, teaching should be in the pupils' own language instead of in English up to the eighth year of schooling. Black children were given a different syllabus from that taught in white schools. Their education was taken out of the control of the Department of Education and put into the hands of the Department of Native Affairs. In that way, those liberal educationists still employed in the Department of Education could have no influence on black schools. The authorities admitted that they were intending to place black children in a permanently inferior position in society.

The 800,000 school places available to black children in 1953 had increased to 1,800,000 by 1963, but a large number of these were situated in the 'homelands'. As a result many parents living in cities had to send their children to the rural homelands for a high school education. The major problem for these parents, however, was that the policy was deliberately designed to limit black advancement and ambition.

*Pupils protesting against the Bantu Education Act. About 7,000 children were expelled from school because of their protests.*

Verwoerd set out his intentions in these words:

What is the use of subjecting a native child to a curriculum which is, in the first instance, traditionally European? What is the use of teaching the Bantu child mathematics when it cannot be used in practice?

If the native is being taught to expect that he will live his adult life under a policy of equal rights, he is making a big mistake.

Verwoerd's speech in Parliament, 17 August 1953

A cartoon showing the effects of Verwoerd's educational policy on blacks.

Verwoerd's education policy went right to the heart of the system – its teachers. Salaries were kept at subsistence level and poorly qualified teachers were employed. In 1954, he stated in the Senate that 'people who believe in equality are not desirable teachers for Natives'. The following year a law was passed forbidding teachers to express their political views. As a result of ignoring this, many teachers were dismissed. Others left teaching of their own accord because they could no longer realise the goals they had set for their pupils. Some had their homes raided by the police. Among the victimised teachers were leading members of the profession. Each year the proportion of high school teachers with university qualifications declined. By 1980, hardly any high school teachers were university graduates.

## Closing the gaps

The State-Aided Institutions Act of 1957 allowed the government to enforce segregation in libraries and places of entertainment. In the Native Laws Amendment Bill of the same year, the government was given the power to ban meetings, classes or even religious services in a 'white' area if they were attended by blacks. By the end of the 1950s, the apartheid system and the laws upholding it were all in place.

## Discussion points

> What damage do you think each of the changes in education did to black communities?

> Why do you think the government wanted to restrict education for black people?

# Legalising the apartheid state

## APARTHEID IN PRACTICE

> Between 1949 and 1959, legislation to separate people was passed by Parliament. Each Act reduced both rights and opportunities for the majority of South Africa's people.

Key aspects of the policy

> Group areas
> Population registration
> Separate education
> Homelands.

## HOMELANDS

These areas were set aside for blacks as places where they would have political rights. This was supposed to justify their exclusion from mainstream politics. The homelands (Bantustans) separated people not only along racial lines, but also into various 'tribal' groupings.

## THE ALL-WHITE VOTERS' ROLL

As soon as he came to power, Malan took their voting rights away from the few black and Indian people who had held them. He, and his successor after him, then went on to remove Coloured people from the voters' roll. By depriving the Coloured people of their right to vote for MPs, a major source of opposition was removed. The Nationalist position became deeply entrenched in society.

## PASSES

Passes were 96-page books which blacks had to carry and show on demand. The books contained information about the holder's address and employment as well as their finger-prints. The passes gave the government a powerful way of controlling where blacks lived and worked.

## GROUP AREAS

The group areas were set up to make people of different races live in different places. Black people were made to leave those urban areas where they lived and were moved to a place chosen by the government. The cleared area would often be bulldozed and replaced by new communities occupied by whites.

## THE BANTU EDUCATION ACT

The Bantu Education Act was designed to make black children inferior to their white counterparts. Black children were educated just enough to work in factories and urban areas. They were encouraged to think of the homelands as where they belonged. They were taught in their mother tongues – and just enough English to communicate with whites. Almost all secondary schools were built in the homelands. In this way the government used education to keep black people out of white areas.

# Opposing apartheid

Apartheid was upheld by the government with the full force of the law. It was both difficult and dangerous to oppose government policy. Nevertheless, many people fought the system in different ways.

## Who opposed apartheid and what means did they use?

Apartheid laws were strictly enforced by the police and by the army. In later years most of the white population came to accept apartheid as the customary way of life and children grew up in a society that considered white supremacy and the separation of the races to be the norm. Christian National Education became the education policy for all white children in the mid-1960s. It was based on the idea that God had created separate nations and that children should be educated within their own nations, separately from other nations. Originally it was supposed to be for Afrikaans-speaking children only, but by the late 1960s, the National Party argued that whites, rather than Afrikaners, composed one nation. It adapted

ideas about Afrikaner culture and taught white children that these were the basic ideas of Western civilisation and culture. In the early 1970s, it set up Youth Preparedness Programmes which encouraged white children to see blacks who opposed apartheid as communists and terrorists. Teachers were told that the child was basically sinful and that it was the job of the teacher, as God's representative, to mould the child to adulthood. This approach encouraged pupils to be passive and uncritical and teachers to be authoritarian.

Not everyone in South Africa, however, readily accepted apartheid. In spite of government measures to stifle opposition, protest and resistance came from many quarters.

### HOW DID THE GOVERNMENT STIFLE OPPOSITION?

All opposition was met with harsh measures by the government and secret police. Political activists were soon arrested and sometimes tortured or murdered. A number met their death by 'falling out of windows' at the headquarters of the secret police. The police usually explained that they were 'attempting to escape'.

Banning orders, which were signed by the Minister of Justice, were a useful tool for the government. They stopped the person named in the order from writing, broadcasting, being quoted, attending meetings, or from leaving a particular area without permission from a magistrate. Any gathering that, in the opinion of the Minister of Justice, might 'seriously endanger public peace' could also be banned, as could any publication or political organisation.

Newspapers opposed to the regime were censored and some were banned. Anyone who wrote articles critical of any aspect of government policy could be prosecuted.

People who were arrested could be detained without trial for 90 days. Later this was extended to 180 days. This frightened many people.

If necessary, the government could always declare a state of emergency. This meant it could ignore any laws that might have prevented heavy-handed or brutal action against its enemies. Many opponents of apartheid fled the country.

## White liberal opposition

Many white people, by legal and illegal means, attempted to oppose apartheid. Helen Suzman, once a Parliamentary member of the United Party and later of the breakaway Democratic Party, was a relentless critic of apartheid in a hostile Parliament for over 30 years.

### SOURCE A

*A former government detainee describes Helen Suzman, who was, for many years, the only parliamentary representative of the white liberal community:*

[She was] the one Member of Parliament whose name is inextricably linked with the only systematic attempt to get international standards implemented in the prisons in general and on Robben Island in particular. Her staunch insistence on the application of humane provisions became quite literally a bridge of survival and of sanity over which most of us could walk out of imprisonment without having been too deeply scarred and disfigured.

Neville Alexander, *Robben Island Dossier*, 1994

### SOURCE B

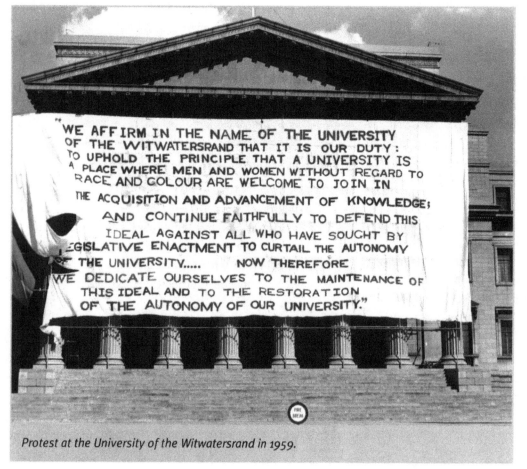

*Protest at the University of the Witwatersrand in 1959.*

> ## THE DEMOCRATIC PARTY
>
> The United Party had never recovered from its defeat by the Nationalists in 1948 so it tried to win more popular support by promoting racist ideas. As a result, in 1959, a group of liberal members broke away and organised themselves into a new party. It had many name changes and its fortunes fluctuated. For many years, its sole representative in Parliament was Helen Suzman. The size of the party did not reflect its importance as the voice of white, liberal conscience. It reached its strongest position in the troubled 1980s, before the liberation movements were unbanned by the government.

Under such conditions, popular protest was made very difficult but it was not entirely suppressed. Thousands of people in Cape Town, Port Elizabeth and Johannesburg had joined the Torch Commando processions of 1952, protesting against the government's intention to remove Coloured voters from the common roll.

An organisation known as the Black Sash Movement was founded in 1955 by a group of white women. At first their intention was to protest against the removal of Coloured voting rights. The members later set up advice centres in order to try to help the blacks in the cities. Many were suffering acute distress at the break-up of their homes because of the enforcement of the Pass Laws.

Many university students, especially from the English-language universities, frequently demonstrated against laws discriminating on the grounds of colour.

Students' protest marches were banned and they were forbidden to demonstrate outside the university grounds. Student protests usually brought a heavy-handed police response.

## The Suppression of Communism Act

The government's Suppression of Communism Act made it even more difficult to oppose the government. Every protest could now be regarded as 'communist inspired' and dealt with severely. During the Cold War between Russia and the West, many people, who might have protested against the government, kept quiet because they were afraid of being called communist. There were popular protests in 1950 when the Bill went through Parliament but they were not well co-ordinated. For most whites, the 1960s were a time of economic growth and increasing prosperity. This tended to lessen criticism of the regime.

## Resistance among blacks

Black people were intimidated by the system and by the way in which it was callously administered. In spite of this, their day-to-day experiences of apartheid were so unpleasant that they were encouraged to resist. The SANC, later the ANC, had continued to encourage peaceful resistance campaigns from 1917 to 1924 and to organise strikes against the colour bar. In 1943, the ANC had founded an active youth league.

## Stay-at-home days

The ANC adopted 'stay-at-home' days in 1951 as part of a civil disobedience campaign. These campaigns were first suggested by Walter Sisulu, Secretary-General of the ANC. He hoped that they would draw attention to the injustice of the system. They involved many people but put few at risk.

In 1952 many protests were organised. In January, Dr Moroka, the President of the ANC, and Mr Sisulu, called on the Prime Minister to repeal the six 'unjust laws' (the Pass Laws, Stock Limitation, which controlled the numbers of cattle which blacks were allowed to own, the Bantu Authorities Act, the Group Areas Act, the Voters Representation Act and the Suppression of Communism Act).

On 6 April, Afrikaner nationalists were enthusiastically celebrating the tercentenary of the arrival of the Dutchman, Jan van Riebeeck, the first governor of the colony, at the Cape of Good Hope in 1652. The black people of South Africa chose to observe a stay-at-home day on this important day for Afrikaners. This was their comment on the government's insensitivity toward the majority of the people.

**SOURCE C**

*A mass demonstration against unjust laws held in Red Square, Fordsburg in April 1952.*

Jurgen Schadeburg

37

## The Defiance Campaign

On 26 June, the ANC began what they called a Defiance Campaign, to make the government's apartheid policy unworkable. Men marched without their passes, ignored curfew laws, walked brazenly through entrances marked 'EUROPEANS ONLY', and stood at 'white' reserved counters in Post Offices. Nelson Mandela, now a member of the National Executive of the ANC, was one of them. The police arrested the protesters for these minor offences. Every arrest made a point about the injustice and pettiness of the laws that had been broken. The campaign succeeded. It put South Africa on the United Nations agenda and, in 1952, the UN General Assembly passed its first resolution condemning apartheid. The campaign spread across the country and received much support in the Eastern Cape. All went well until October when, after serious rioting in the cities of Port Elizabeth and East London, the protest movement began to die down. In both places, violence broke out after the police intervened. These incidents highlighted the hard-line attitude of the authorities and the strength of the pent-up feelings of the protesters. Six whites and 26 blacks were killed in the riots (including a Catholic nun) and buildings were torched. The authorities took advantage of the fear and outrage among whites to come down hard on the entire movement. Over 8,400 people were arrested and nearly 8,000 of them convicted. The government passed the Criminal Law Amendment and the Public Safety Act, which gave them even more control over protesters.

One of the last protest campaigns of 1952 was led by Patrick Duncan, son of a former Governor-General of South Africa, and Manilal, son of Mahatma Gandhi.

## Opposition to the Bantu Education Act

Teacher opposition to the Bantu Education Act of 1953 was immediate. The government immediately dismissed teachers who objected. In May 1954, the ANC announced its opposition to the Act. The Women's League, the Youth League, the Congress Alliance and the Liberal Party decided that black children should boycott the schools. Volunteer teachers would provide alternative education. On 12 April, thousands of children stayed away from school in order to march in protest with their parents. The Minister announced that children who were not back at school by 25 April, would receive no further education. It forced most parents to adopt the 'some education is better than no education' approach, but a long and bitter battle over education had begun.

## Bus boycotts

From 1957 to 1959 there were a number of bus boycotts, when thousands of blacks walked 48 kilometres (30 miles) a day to work and back for three months, rather than accept increased fares. The supposed issue was the rising cost of living, but the real grievance was against a system which gave working men and women little control over their lives.

SOURCE D

*Blacks who were fortunate enough to afford the taxi fare queuing for taxis into the city during the bus boycotts.*

## Protests against passes

The pass system was bitterly resented. Protest flared up when, in 1956, the government announced that, in future, women would also have to carry passes. After months of campaigning against this law, the Federation of South African Women (FSAW), whose president was a black woman, Lilian Ngoyi, and whose secretary was a white social worker, Helen Joseph, decided to mount a large demonstration. On 27 October 1955, 2,000 women protested in Pretoria. Their support grew, and on 9 August 1956, 20,000 women of all races took a petition to the Prime Minister.

### SOURCE E

*One of the leaders, Frances Baard, tells us:*

Early the next morning we set off. We proceeded in groups of twos and threes, silently. We could not sing or shout slogans because that would constitute a gathering and a march and we would open ourselves to police action. We set off for the Union Buildings around 12 o'clock. And, by half past two, the only piece of ground that was visible was the gravel terrace leading up to the stairway.

### SOURCE G

*Women protesting at the Pass Laws.*

The Prime Minister was not there to receive the petition. They left their petitions outside his empty office. The women stood in silence for 30 minutes, then sang *Nkosi Sikelel' iAfrika* [God Bless Africa] and dispersed singing 'Now you have touched the women, you have struck a rock, you will be crushed'.

### SOURCE F

Jurgen Schadeburg

*Women delivering petitions against Pass Laws to the Prime Minister in Pretoria in October 1955. Pictured here left to right are Sophie Williams, Helen Joseph, Lilian Ngoyi, and Rahima Moosa, one woman representing each racial group.*

## The Freedom Charter

The Defiance Campaign widened the support for the ANC. In June 1955, the leaders of all the anti-apartheid movements decided to call a Congress of the People at Kliptown (near Johannesburg). It was attended by a non-racial group of 3,000. A charter was produced for discussion by the assembled people. The police arrived, confiscated all documents, and took the names and addresses of many of those present. The congress, nevertheless, resulted in the Freedom Charter. It set out the guiding objectives of the movement, and demanded a non-racial, democratic government with equality for all before the law. It became, in time, a much-cherished manifesto.

### SOURCE H

*A delegation at Kliptown.*

### SOURCE I

### THE FREEDOM CHARTER

> *Clause 1, The People Shall Govern,* affirms the right of all, regardless of race, colour or sex, to vote;

> *Clause 2, All National Groups Shall Have Equal Rights,* affords equality before the law, in schools, and forbids racial insults;

> *Clause 3, The People Shall Share in the Country's Wealth,* calls for the nationalisation of the mines, banks and industrial monopolies, and for all people to have equal economic and job rights;

> *Clause 4, The Land Shall Be Shared among Those Who Work It,* demands a redistribution of the land, as well as the abolition of any restrictions on movements of people, access to land, and stock holdings;

> *Clause 5, All Shall Be Equal before the Law,* promises the abolition of detentions or bannings without trial, as well as all discriminatory laws;

> *Clause 6, All Shall Enjoy Human Rights,* guarantees freedom of speech, worship, and association, and unfettered freedom of movement;

> *Clause 7, There Shall Be Work and Security,* recognises the right of all to work and to equal pay for equal work, lays down minimum working conditions, and promises the abolition of child labour;

> *Clause 8, The Doors of Learning and Culture Shall Be Opened,* sets out principles of free, universal, compulsory and equal education, promises to wipe out illiteracy, and undertakes to remove all cultural, sporting and educational colour bars;

> *Clause 9, There Shall Be Houses, Security and Comfort,* promises decent housing for all, the demolition of slums and fenced townships, proper medical care for all as well as care of the aged, the disabled and orphans;

> *Clause 10, There Shall Be Peace and Friendship,* says South Africa will respect the rights of other states and will strive for world peace.

The Freedom Charter concludes: *'Let all who love their people and their country now say, as we say here: these freedoms we will fight for, side by side, throughout our lives until we have won our liberty.'*

## The treason trials

The police made good use of the information they gathered at the congress. In a dawn swoop, on 5 December 1956, they arrested 156 people of all races including the leaders of the Indian community and most of the leaders of the ANC. They were all charged with treason. The state, however, found it difficult to prove the charges. After a trial which dragged on for almost five years every one of the accused was acquitted.

## Political alliances

During this time of widespread popular protest, the various movements that supported a non-racial policy joined together to form political alliances. In 1953, the ANC forged links with the Congress of Democrats, the South African Indian Congress and the South African Coloured People's Organisation. But the African Nationalists, or Africanists, in the ranks of the ANC, began expressing other ideas. They objected to the Freedom Charter on the grounds that South Africa should not belong to 'all who live in it' but to those who could be termed 'Africans'. They thought that the ANC should be a black African movement. In 1959, the Africanists founded a new party – the Pan Africanist Congress (PAC). Its leader was Robert Sobukwe.

---

### PAN AFRICANIST CONGRESS (PAC)

This movement was founded on African nationalist principles. Sobukwe defined an African as one who gives his loyalty to Africa, but later the word was given a stricter, more racial, definition. Sobukwe was arrested at the Sharpeville massacre in 1960 and was sent to Robben Island. He died in 1978. The PAC was banned together with the ANC in 1960. Members of the movement in exile helped to publicise the condition of South Africa, and its armed wing attacked random targets. Its adoption of the slogan 'one settler, one bullet' before the 1994 elections did not gain it many votes. It received only 1.25 per cent of the vote in the elections.

---

## >> Activity

1 Why was it difficult to oppose authority in South Africa in the 1950s?

2 How did the following people oppose apartheid:
   a white liberals,
   b black people?

3 Which issues were universal problems for working-class people, and which were problems particularly South African?

4 Read the Freedom Charter carefully. Why do you think supporters of apartheid disliked this document?

5 Opposition leaders called for a non-violent campaign. Why do you think some protests became violent?

# Sharpeville

In 1960 there was a massacre in Sharpeville. This was considered to be a turning point in the modern history of South Africa.

## Why were the events of 21 March 1960 so significant?

The two rival opposition organisations, the ANC and the PAC, began to compete for supporters. The ANC called for a one-day protest against the Pass Laws on 31 March 1960. The PAC then called for a more forceful protest on 21 March and suggested that protesters should march on police stations to demonstrate their objections.

Most of the protests passed off peacefully, but at Sharpeville a confrontation between police and marchers ended in tragedy. Some police opened fire, scattering the protesters in a hail of bullets. In the chaos and confusion that resulted, 69 people died and many more were wounded. Many of them had been shot in the back.

**SOURCE A**

*Protesters flee from the bullets.*

**SOURCE B**

*The scene after the shootings.*

**SOURCE C**

*An eye-witness recalls:*

Most of the bodies were strewn on the road running through the field where we were. One man who had been lying still, dazedly got to his feet, staggered a few yards and then fell in a heap. One by one the guns stopped. More than 200 Africans were shot down. The police said that the crowd was armed with 'ferocious weapons' which littered the compound after they fled. I saw no weapons. I saw only shoes, hats and a few bicycles left among the bodies.

Humphrey Tyler, *Nelson Mandela and the Rise of the ANC*, 1960

## SOURCE D

*The funerals of those killed by the police in Sharpeville on 21 March 1960.*

Jurgen Schadeburg

## Widespread riots

In Cape Town, too, there were clashes between the protesters and the police, which led to widespread rioting. The government seemed astonished by how fierce the opposition was and suspended arrests for pass offences. Overnight, South Africa became the focus of world-media attention. Albert Luthuli, the head of the ANC, who later that year received the Nobel Peace Prize, publicly burned his pass. Eighteen thousand people were arrested. Cape Town leader, Philip Kgosana, was arrested when he kept an appointment with the Minister of Justice to discuss grievances.

## SOURCE E

*Luthuli receiving the Nobel Peace Prize for 1961 in Oslo. It was awarded for his work to promote tolerance and understanding among the races.*

## SOURCE F

*Africans burning their passes after Sharpeville.*

By the end of the month, however, the government regained its confidence and declared the ANC and the PAC banned organisations. The ANC was to became the most influential underground organisation under the leadership of Oliver Tambo.

## The consequences of Sharpeville

The events at Sharpeville led to the worldwide condemnation of apartheid. It was the beginning of a widespread protest campaign outside South Africa. The economy was affected by these dramatic events. In the next 18 months R248 million left South Africa. The gold and foreign reserves plummeted from R351 million to R142 million. This set-back for the government was surprisingly short-lived, however. The country was about to enter a period of prosperity which dulled a great deal of opposition from within South Africa.

>> Activity

1 Explain in your own words what happened in Sharpeville.

2 Why do you think Sharpeville was so important in the history of the fight against apartheid?

# The state grows in confidence

The struggles of the resistance seemed to be in vain. By the time of Prime Minister Strijdom's death in 1958, Verwoerd had become the obvious man to succeed him. He survived an assassination attempt in 1961 and remained Prime Minister until 1966, when he was assassinated in the House of Assembly by a parliamentary messenger. By 1961, he was reaching the height of his power. Internal opposition had been stifled and the policy of apartheid continued to be further refined. British firms were trading with and investing in South Africa. Germany, France, Japan and the USA were all involved in trade with South Africa by the late 1960s. Those who were opposed to the South African government's apartheid policy had little reason to be optimistic.

Prime Minister Verwoerd addressing a meeting of his supporters in 1961.

## THE WIND OF CHANGE

In 1960, a few weeks before the Sharpeville shootings, the British Prime Minister, Harold Macmillan had arrived on a visit to South Africa at the end of his African tour. On 2 February he made his famous 'Wind of change' speech to the dismay and anger of the white nationalists in the South African Parliament.

'The most striking of all the impressions I have formed since I left London a month ago is the strength of this African consciousness. In different places it may take different forms, but it is happening everywhere. The wind of change is blowing through the continent. Whether we like it or not, this growth of political consciousness is a political fact.

As a fellow member of the Commonwealth it is our earnest desire to give South Africa our support and encouragement, but I hope you won't mind my saying frankly that there are some aspects of your policies which make it impossible for us to do this without being false to our own deep convictions about the political destinies of free men, to which in our territories we are trying to give effect.'

Verwoerd's response was that 'This is our motherland. We have nowhere else to go.'

## The Republic

Many Afrikaners wanted South Africa to become a republic both to regain what they had lost in the Boer War and to loosen the ties with Britain. Verwoerd was determined to make this long-cherished Afrikaner dream possible. A small but decisive majority in an all white referendum voted that South Africa should become a republic.

Therefore, on 31 May 1961, South Africa withdrew from the Commonwealth and declared itself a republic.

*C.R. Swart is sworn in as the first President of the republic of South Africa. Verwoerd is on the left of the picture.*

### WHY WAS SOUTH AFRICA ABLE TO RESIST CHANGE FOR SO LONG?

> South Africa was economically strong between 1960 and 1970.
> Countries around the world continued to trade with and to invest in South Africa.
> South Africa had the support of the neighbouring colonial powers in Africa, such as Portugal, until 1975.
> During the Cold War, countries in the West felt that they needed support from South Africa against the Soviet Union. South Africa's geographical position on the sea route from the oil fields of the Gulf to the West would be of strategic importance if war broke out with the Soviet Union.
> South African intelligence forces had strong links with the CIA and the US Defence Department.
> South Africa was a vital source of minerals for the USA and Europe. Particularly important was the fact that it was a major source of uranium for the US nuclear industry.

### Discussion points

> After Sharpeville, the South African government became even more unpopular around the world. Why do you think this did not persuade them to change their minds about apartheid?

> Why did Western countries do little in practical terms to undermine apartheid?

# Protest becomes violent

## The armed wing

By 1961, the government had rejected protest, petitions and attempts at dialogue. Albert Luthuli was restricted to his home in Natal. It was felt that the time for non-violent defiance was over. Mandela went underground and helped to establish *Umkhonto We Sizwe* (Spear of the Nation), known as MK, the military wing of the ANC. A white student group called the African Resistance Movement was founded for the same purpose. The PAC created Poqo – a military wing dedicated to terror as a means of weakening the government. The first ANC act of sabotage was carried out on 16 December 1961 (the anniversary of the Afrikaner victory over the Zulus at Blood River), a sacred day in Afrikaner history.

## The arrest of Mandela

The resistance movement suffered a severe blow in August 1962 when Mandela, who had earned the title 'Black Pimpernel', was arrested. He was posing, at the time, as a driver to Cecil Williams, a white member of Umkhonto We Sizwe (MK). They were driving through Natal engrossed in plans for sabotage when, in Mandela's

## MASS POLICE ALERT AFTER TEN BOMB EXPLOSIONS

Every available policeman in the country was on duty last night after Saturday night's ten bomb explosions that rocked the Rand and Port Elizabeth. The explosions are believed by the police to be the first phase of a terrorist campaign against *apartheid*.

The *Cape Times*, 18 December 1961

words, 'I noticed a Ford V-8 filled with white men shoot past us on the right. I instinctively turned round to look behind and I saw two more cars filled with white men. Suddenly, in front of us, the Ford was signalling us to stop. I knew in that instant that my life on the run was over.'

In October 1962, the first of the 'Free Mandela' campaigns was launched – such campaigns would continue for almost 30 years.

## The Rivonia trials

A year later, many leading members of the ANC and the MK, the South African Indian Congress, the South African Coloured People's Organisation and the Congress of Democrats were arrested while they were attending a secret meeting at Rivonia, the secret headquarters of the MK, near Johannesburg. They were charged with treason. After a trial which lasted over four years they were found guilty, and sentenced to life imprisonment.

*Protesters demanding the release of Nelson Mandela.*

Those arrested at Rivonia were Walter Sisulu, Govan Mbeki, Raymond Mahlaba, Ahmed Kathrada, Lionel Bernstein and Bob Hepple. Information collected at Rivonia led the police to Dennis Goldberg, Arthur Goldreich and Harold Wolpe. Nelson Mandela was put on trial with them. They were defended by Bram Fischer, an Afrikaner, who would later be jailed for his anti-apartheid activities.

The accused were able to make clear to the world's press during the trial exactly why they had acted in this way. Messages poured in from supporters all over the world. The intense interest, both inside and outside South Africa, probably saved the defendants from the death sentence. The resistance leaders who escaped arrest fled into exile but the ANC, MK and Poqo were no longer able to operate effectively within South Africa.

A member of the African Resistance Movement, called John Harris, exploded a bomb in the concourse of the Johannesburg Railway Station. One woman was killed and another was badly injured. Harris was tried and executed.

## Discussion point

> Why do you think the ANC turned to violence in 1961?

### NELSON MANDELA'S DEFENCE AT THE TRIAL

At the outset I want to say that the suggestion made by the state in its opening [statement] that the struggle in South Africa is under the influence of foreigners or Communists is wholly incorrect. I have done whatever I did, both as an individual and as a leader of my people, because of my experience in South Africa, and my own proudly felt African background.

We felt that without sabotage there would be no way open to the African people to succeed in their struggle against the principle of white supremacy. All lawful modes of expressing opposition to this principle had been closed by legislation and we were placed in a position in which we had either to accept a permanent state of inferiority or to defy the government. We chose to defy the government.

# BOMB HORROR

## *Victims in flames on concourse*

STAFF REPORTER

A TIME-BOMB exploded in the giant concourse of Johannesburg's railway yesterday afternoon, injuring at least 23 people.

Anonymous telephone calls tipped off newspapers about the blast minutes before it happened.

The bomb went off as hundreds of travellers crowded the concourse at the start of the rush hour. It had been left in a suitcase beneath the bench of a small waiting room.

Six people were described last night as "very ill" after the blast, and a seventh was said to be "serious". The very ill patients include two small girls and a 77-year-old woman, Mrs E. Rhys. A three-year-old boy was taken to the Children's Hospital in a critical condition.

Nine people were discharged, and one admitted to a private nursing home. The rest of the 23 injured people were treated for shock, cuts and burns.

People ran screaming with clothing on fire as flaming petrol was flung out of the cubicle in the blast. Most of the victims were burnt. Others were lacerated by flying glass.

The explosion erupted from the cubicle above platform No.5 and No.6 at 4.33 p.m. Four people in the cubicle were horribly burnt.

Blue flames engulfed them as they staggered into the Whites only concourse, and smoke filled the building.

As women screamed, Railway First Aid men and volunteers swung into action. Passersby beat out and smothered the flames. Victims were given emergency treatment at a chemist's shop on the station, at the Railway Police charge office, and in a concourse bookshop.

Twelve ambulances and private cars took them to hospital. Five officers directed the operation with walkie-talkie radio, and scores of police moved in to keep the crowds clear.

Ninety minutes after the explosion the Minister of Justice, Mr. Verster, arrived.

## *MINUTES LATER: THE DAMAGE*

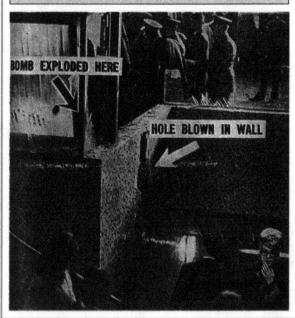

BOMB EXPLODED HERE

HOLE BLOWN IN WALL

*Bomb at the Johannesburg Railway Station, Rand Daily Mail, 25 July 1964.*

# Youthful resistance

Young people in South Africa have played a special and often leading role in the campaign against apartheid.

## Why were the actions of young people so significant?

### Student protest

The English-language universities played an important role in keeping liberal, non-racial ideals alive. The non-racial National Union of South African Students (NUSAS) continued to protest at the injustices of apartheid in a country that was becoming more and more isolated from world opinion.

### The Black Consciousness Movement

During the late 1960s, the Black Consciousness Movement was gaining in popularity. This was a movement that arose because of the political frustrations of blacks. It centred around the idea that blacks should gain confidence in their ability to change things for themselves, end their dependence on whites, and win their own freedom. The movement was influenced by the writings of the Algerian, Frantz Fanon, the black power movement in the USA and the international student revolts of the late 1960s. In 1969, black students broke away from NUSAS to form the South African

Students' Organisation (SASO). This was an organisation for black students. Steve Biko, the young medical student who had founded SASO, said that blacks needed to be aware of their own identity and 'not regard themselves as appendages to white society'. He thought SASO would be more successful than NUSAS had been in encouraging black students to support the principles of the Black Consciousness Movement. In 1972, the Black People's Convention was founded to promote the work of political groups in sympathy with Biko's ideas.

### SOURCE B

*When later describing the uprising of 1976, one student, B. Masethla, said:*

Bantu Education had decreed that we should be nothing. We were determined to rise above it, using whatever means we could.

In 1976, when it seemed that the government had crushed all significant opposition, people suddenly erupted in a fury of outrage and anguish. The issue that provoked these riots was education but, as on previous occasions, many other grievances lay behind the violence that followed.

Many of the young black people blamed their inadequate education for the fact that they were unemployed, and the apartheid policy for the acute housing shortage.

The event that caused this violent outbreak of protest was a government announcement that half the school curriculum, including Mathematics and Science, would in future be taught only in Afrikaans. Teachers would, therefore, be made to teach in a language that many of them did not speak and that pupils did not understand. The South African Students Movement (SASM) organised a demonstration for 16 June 1976.

### SOURCE A

Students marching with placards in Soweto.

## The Soweto riots

The march in the black township of Soweto started peacefully, but police shot dead a boy of 13 and a bloody confrontation followed. Once the violence began, the demonstration turned into a riot. The pupils stoned vehicles and attacked whites who worked in Soweto.

## SOURCE C

*An eye-witness describes the scene:*

Twice the group of police tried to stop the procession. One policeman shot a boy who fell. I think he was dead. At that moment the children spread out and picked up stones. They started throwing stones at the police. Then the other policemen fired with revolvers at the children and seven more were hit by bullets. The dead boy was Hector Peterson.

Clive Emdon, *Rand Daily Mail*, 17 June 1976

## SOURCE D

*Mbuyisa Makhubu carrying Hector Peterson accompanied by Hector's sister Antoinette.*

## SOURCE E

The story of the boy who picked up and carried Hector is part of a wider tragedy – the flight of young people into exile. The boy's mother tells us that her son, Mbuyisa Makhubu, was in his grandmother's house when he heard the first shots. He ran out of the house and as he approached the crowd, Hector fell at his feet. Mbuyisa was on the run from that day onward. He left the country two months later. His mother received letters from Botswana and Nigeria. The last letter arrived in 1978. She has not heard from him since, and assumes that he died in exile.

*New Nation*, June 1986

## SOURCE F

# From demo to killer riot – hour by hour

Staff reporter

THIS is a step-by-step account of Soweto's day of death and destruction:

**7–9.30 am** – Groups of high school children move from school to school carrying placards and demonstrating outside schools against the use of Afrikaans as a medium of instruction.

**9.30 am** – By this time a crowd estimated by the police to be 4000 to 5000 strong has a confrontation with a small police group which tries to stop the procession and take away the placards.

This leads to the stoning of police and a shooting incident in which a boy of 13 is killed and seven children reported injured from gunfire.

About the same time Dr Melville Edelstein, a sociologist, is killed at the Morris Isaacson High School.

All police are withdrawn from the area – in the vicinity of Orlando West High School.

**10 am** – A WRAB official is clubbed to death in the same vicinity where the main group of youths has collected.

The Black municipal policeman with him is knocked unconcious and the vehicle he is in set alight. He dies in the fire.

**10–12.30 pm** – Throughout the morning the Orlando police station is used as an operational headquarters. However, a large group of police takes up positions near the Orlando station overlooking the hill where the Orlando West High School is situated, and calls for reinforcements.

Ammunition supplies are brought in and Army helicopters are called for.

**1.30 pm** – Two Army helicopters arrive and overfly the Orlando West High School dropping teargas to disperse crowds of youths.

A number of vehicles are set alight in the vicinity and a cloud of smoke billows on the hill. Police are able to remove the bodies of the dead WRAB official and the municipal policeman.

The riot squad from Johannesburg is moved into the Morris Isaacson High School vicinity on an adjacent range of hills to the west.

**2 pm** – New fires break out in the vicinity of the Phefeni station and more police reinforcements are sent in.

**2.30 pm** – A column of police vehicles and men moves off from the area of the Orlando station on to the hill situation of the Orlando West high school. They find most of the huge crowd of youths has dispersed.

**3 pm** – Large groups of youths are reported to be moving about in different areas, stoning cars. A police anti-terrorist force from Johannesburg in camouflage suits and armed with light machine guns arrive. They are sent into the area of the Phefeni station.

The WRAB buildings at Dube and Jabulani are set alight, and by this time a total of 36 burning and wrecked cars are found on the roads. A beer lorry is set alight near the Jabulani police station.

**3–4 pm** – New groups of armed police arrive at the Orlando police station and are deployed into different areas. Police use teargas in the vicinity of the WRAB offices of Dube and Jabulani to disperse crowds of youths.

**4–5 pm** – Police officers in control are receiving reports of new fires breaking out in White City and a number of other areas.

**5–8 pm** – Police receive reports that at least 20 buildings have been set alight including the Urban Bantu Council building. Widespread looting of shops and bottle stores are reported. New units of armed police arrive from different parts of the Witwatersrand.

**8.30 pm** – Two Black police report an attack on their car on the east side of the Orlando police station on the road into Soweto. Rioters make attempts to set fire to a garage and bottle store on the boundary between Soweto and Noordgesig.

**9.30–10 pm** – Fourteen Hippo armoured personnel carriers arrive and move off carrying police units for patrols of the worst hit areas. A group of 13 youths arrested by the police are brought into the Orlando police station.

*Rand Daily Mail*, Thursday 17 June 1976

When they heard the news from Soweto, white students made protests. Some from the University of the Witwatersrand ignored police orders and marched in protest. The police charged them. The actions of the South African government were condemned throughout the world. The criticism, on this occasion, did not die down as quickly as it had done after similar incidents.

## SOURCE G

*The students from Witwatersrand did not only face opposition from the police:*

White railway workers, whose livelihood depended on apartheid's job reservation were quick to join in the attack on the students who were fleeing from the police. Some of the fleeing students scrambled down the railway embankment and ran across the tracks toward the Johannesburg station. They were caught by workers who kicked and punched them before pushing them over the fence into the arms of the waiting police.

*Cape Times,* 18 June 1976

The rioting and demonstrations continued for weeks but, in the end, the government managed to gain control of the situation inside the country.

## The death of Steve Biko

On 18 August 1977 Steve Biko of the Black Consciousness Movement was detained. He was dead within 26 days. He had been kept naked in a cell and so badly beaten up that he went into a coma. These injuries, and their neglect while in prison, resulted in his death. In that same year 17 organisations and two newspapers were banned. Resistance seemed futile, the government, backed by a powerful army and police force, appeared invincible.

## SOURCE H

**Hundreds demonstrate at SA London embassy**

*A photograph and newspaper headline from the* Cape Times, *18 June 1976. The police baton-charged white students who were protesting about the events in Soweto. Other protests around the world included a large demonstration in London.*

## AZANIAN PEOPLE'S ORGANISATION (AZAPO)

In 1978, a new organisation was formed that held similar views to the other organisations inspired by the Black Consciousness Movement. It promoted strong Africanist and socialist ideas and was anxious to spread black consciousness throughout the working classes. AZAPO established links with the trade union movement, which was determined to overthrow the apartheid regime.

In 1977, Prime Minister B. J. Vorster, Verwoerd's successor, called an election. The Nationalists achieved their most convincing victory and won 134 seats while the opposition parties only won 30 between them. But the events of 1976 had changed South Africa for ever. Although people were not aware of it at the time, the government was now on the defensive.

## >> Activity

**1** How and why did young people lead the fight against apartheid in 1976?

# Resisting apartheid

## HOW PEOPLE RESISTED APARTHEID

> Stay-at-home days

> Protest marches

> Petitions

> Refusing to obey unjust laws

> Deliberately risking arrest for petty offences

> Armed resistance and sabotage

> Women's groups

> Children's protest

> White liberal opposition in Parliament

> Anti-apartheid organisations

## ANTI-APARTHEID GROUPS AND ORGANISATIONS

**The Black Sash** was a group of dedicated women who tried to help victims of apartheid, particularly with legal queries. They demonstrated opposition to unjust laws even when this became illegal.

**The Institute of Race Relations** was a liberal organisation which recorded and publicised events of the apartheid years.

**The Liberal Party** was founded in 1953. It advocated equality for all but was disbanded in 1968 when it was forbidden to have a non-racial membership.

**The Democratic Party** was the voice of white liberal opposition to apartheid. For many years its only representative in Parliament, Helen Suzman, spoke out against apartheid and in support of the many people who had been unjustly imprisoned.

**The Federation of South African Women** was a group of women of all races who organised petitions, and protests against the Pass Laws.

### THE SIGNIFICANCE OF THE FREEDOM CHARTER

This document called for basic human rights for all South Africans and had as its foundation the ideals of non-racism and non-sexism.

### SHARPEVILLE

This revealed the level of frustration among the people and the level of fear amongst officials of the state. It created worldwide awareness of and revulsion to South Africa's policies.

### THE IMPORTANCE OF THE EDUCATION ISSUE

Education was a key issue. The strength of the opposition to the government's education policy was crucial. It prevented the government from fully carrying out its policy and made it impossible for it to control the levels of violence and wipe out resistance.

## HOW THE GOVERNMENT SUPPRESSED PROTEST

> Imprisonment without trial

> Torture

> Banning

> House arrest

> Murder

> Use of armed force

> Declaring a State of Emergency which allowed it to operate outside the law

# The regime weakens

## Increasing isolation

Throughout the 1960s there was growing pressure on South Africa to change her apartheid policies. Anti-apartheid groups around the world had organised demonstrations and urged that all countries should support trade and sporting boycotts against South Africa. Newly independent black nations in Africa began to join the United Nations, so that organisation became increasingly critical of South Africa's apartheid policy. In 1963, the new Organisation of African Unity made the abolition of apartheid in South Africa one of its main aims. This policy was clearly set out in a document issued in 1969, the Lusaka Manifesto.

### SOUTH WEST AFRICA

After the First World War, the League of Nations let South Africa control the former German colony of South West Africa. When Malan came to power, his apartheid laws were introduced in South West Africa. Its indigenous people, however, wanted independence for the territory which they called Namibia.

In 1960, the South West African People's Organisation (SWAPO) was formed to fight for independence. It was the beginning of an armed struggle, mainly conducted in the northern part of the territory. Over the next ten years the United Nations passed a series of resolutions calling on South Africa to give up the mandate. South Africa attracted increasing criticism over her actions but the government stubbornly refused, and SWAPO intensified its activities.

## Angola

By the mid-1970s, the support South Africa had received from the friendly white governments along the South African border began to collapse. In 1974, Portugal gave independence to her former colonies of Angola and Mozambique. The situation in Angola soon became chaotic, with three black nationalist groups fighting each other for control of the country. Civil war broke out in Angola between groups known as UNITA and the MPLA.

### SOUTH AFRICA AND HER NEIGHBOURS IN THE 1960S

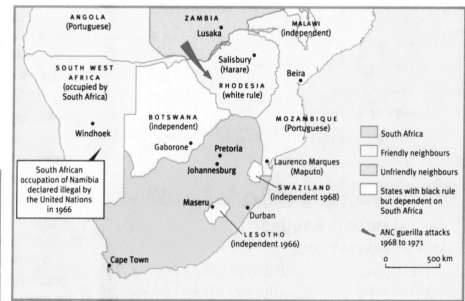

### SOUTHERN AFRICA IN THE 1980S

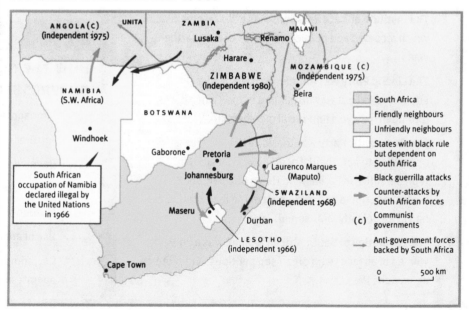

## Military action by South Africa

This new situation in Angola had serious implications for South Africa, especially as the ANC was able to set up bases in Angola and Mozambique within easy reach of Johannesburg and Pretoria. The South West African People's Organisation (SWAPO), which was steadily gaining popular support within South West Africa, was also using bases in southern Angola from which to plan its campaign to liberate Namibia from South African control. South Africa, therefore, decided to become involved in military action beyond its borders. It sent troops to Angola to assist UNITA in its war against the MPLA. Such a move by South Africa would have an added advantage – South African forces would be able to destroy SWAPO's bases in southern Angola. An incursion was launched in October 1975. It came up against well-equipped Cuban troops and failed in both its objectives. Instead, more and more troops were drawn into a campaign to hunt down SWAPO guerrillas and assist UNITA in its ongoing struggle with the MPLA government.

The outcome was a costly, drawn-out stalemate which could be ended only with the granting of independence to Namibia.

## Rhodesia

In 1965 the Labour government in Britain refused to grant Southern Rhodesia independence unless they shared power with the black majority. Ian Smith, the Prime Minister of Rhodesia, declared independence without the consent of the British government. This action became known as the Unilateral Declaration of Independence (UDI). In response to this, the United Nations imposed economic sanctions on Rhodesia. South Africa continued to allow vital supplies, including oil, to be sent to Rhodesia – a move that was widely criticised.

The white-dominated government of Ian Smith was, however, finally forced to hand over power to the black majority after the election of 1980. Robert Mugabe and his ZANU party, bitterly hostile to South Africa, won an overwhelming victory at the polls and Mugabe became Prime Minister of Southern Rhodesia, now renamed Zimbabwe. South Africa lost another friendly state. Black majority rule was established in yet another country in Africa.

*Namibians protesting at the trial of six SWAPO members in Windhoek, Namibia.*

## Internal revolt – the problems of the government

In 1978, a corruption scandal amongst government officials forced the Prime Minister, Vorster, to resign. The scandal discredited the government still further.

The next Prime Minister was P. W. Botha. He could not afford to ignore the fury of the 1976 riots or the anger of the black community. Nor could the increasing opposition to apartheid from outside South Africa be brushed off any longer. Botha saw the need to rethink the apartheid policy. He consequently warned whites to 'adapt or die'. Although he saw the need for reform, he was afraid to appear weak. He was worried that, if reforms were introduced, there would be a backlash from the right-wing extremists in his party.

## Total Strategy

Botha drew up a plan of action known as 'Total Strategy' by which he hoped he could solve South Africa's problems. On the one hand he tried to give the security forces more power to deal more effectively with the opposition from outside South Africa's borders. On the other, he tried to remove some grievances that could be exploited by revolutionaries inside and outside South Africa. He therefore introduced some reforms intended to win the hearts and minds of the blacks. These reforms, as he feared, had the effect of alienating the right-wing of his party, who broke away from the National Party in 1982.

## Changes that challenged the power structure

Botha's government was operating in a South Africa that was very different from that of 1948. The nature of its economy had changed. Gold-mining and farming were not as important as they had been in earlier years. The government no longer had to make sure that a supply of cheap labour was available for these industries. In the 1970s, it was the newer industries that needed labour. They had begun to suffer from a shortage of skilled and semi-skilled workers. The apartheid system, however, had prevented the growth of a skilled labour force. The interests of Afrikaner business were becoming the same as those of any other members of the business community.

The kind of support on which the government depended was changing. Class division seemed to be becoming more important than ethnic division. Hard-line Afrikaners began to support the Conservative Party formed by Andries Treurnicht in 1982. By then, it was the more moderate Afrikaners who supported the National Party and they were joined by many English-speaking people.

The government had to consider that it would have to make alliances with new sections of the community. Behind the scenes, some members from Botha's Cabinet began to make contact with the imprisoned Nelson Mandela.

*President Botha visits Soweto in an effort to reassure white and black communities about reform. He was the first South African Prime Minister to have visited the township.*

### Discussion points

> Why do you think South Africa was criticised for her actions in South West Africa?

> Why did the changes that occurred in Angola and Southern Rhodesia during the 1970s and 1980s weaken the position of the South African government?

> Why was Botha's government forced to consider changes within South Africa?

# The forces for change

Under the leadership of P.W. Botha, the government of South Africa began to make concessions.

## What made Botha's government relax its attitude to apartheid?

### Trade unions

The trade unions became a significant force for social change in the 1970s. Black workers began to realise the power that strike action could give them. Labour and management began to learn how to negotiate and compromise with each other. The unions did not confront the government directly. Instead they began a campaign to persuade international companies to put economic pressure on the South African government.

In the late 1970s some of the unions formed federations. The first one was the non-racial Federation of South African Trade Unions (FOSATU). Then came the exclusively black federations: the Council of Unions of South Africa (CUSA) and the Black Allied Workers' Union (BAWU). They were powerful organisers of industrial and political action. Marches and strikes became an everyday occurrence.

### International sanctions

The ANC and the unions both campaigned for companies to stop investing in South Africa and for countries to boycott South African goods. These international sanctions began to take effect. The government realised that it could no longer resist change. In 1979, Botha met with the leaders of big business and formal links were set up between business leaders and the National Party. He promised to support free enterprise and reform. Gradually the regulations that had reserved jobs for particular racial groups fell into disuse. The more obviously racist aspects of apartheid began to fall away. Pass Laws began to be relaxed. Industry now needed a settled workforce, not a migrant one. More semi-skilled black labour was also needed and that would mean providing a better education for blacks.

More money was spent on black education and urban renewal, but the old thinking did not change readily. The programme of forced removals and of physically separating racial groups continued as before. It seemed as if the government was only interested in cosmetic change.

### The ultra right-wing

Botha's reforms were slowed down by the opposition of new right-wing groups opposed to change. In 1982, the ultra right-wing had broken away from the National Party to form the Conservative Party under Dr A. Treurnicht. More alarming was the fact that new parliamentary groups, even further to the right, like the Afrikaner Resistance Movement (AWB), were created.

**SOURCE A**

*Eugene Terre'blanche, the leader of the AWB, addresses a meeting in 1994.*

## Constitutional reform

In spite of opposition from the right-wing, the government introduced a scheme to bring Coloureds and Indians into parliament. A new parliament was set up that had three assemblies – one for whites, one for Coloureds and one for Indians. This infuriated the black majority, who had been left out of the new political arrangements, but it, nevertheless, marked a shift in the attitude and policy of the ruling party.

## Further economic problems

Economic problems put further pressure on Botha's troubled government. A devastating drought pushed up the price of food. The black homelands turned into disaster areas and desperately needed help from the government. This came at a time when the government was spending a huge amount on weapons and the armed forces, and the price of gold had fallen to $300 an ounce from its 1980 peak of $850 an ounce.

## Increasing pressure from trade unions and resistance organisations

During the mid-1980s, the trade unions and the resistance movements increased their pressure on the government. Members of the ANC returned in secret to help the local resistance in the townships. They began to attack military and police installations. Pupils boycotted schools to try to force the government to restructure their education. The slogan 'Liberation before Education' became their inspiration.

## The United Democratic Front

The ANC-in-exile knew that if protest were to be effective, it needed to be properly co-ordinated. It found the answer in the United Democratic Front (UDF). This non-racial organisation was founded in 1983, in Cape Town. Its membership grew to two million people of all races, with the single aim of abolishing apartheid. The membership included 586 political, religious, trade union, youth league, civic and women's groups. It was able to increase the already very high number of people actively protesting against apartheid. The UDF accepted the Freedom Charter and became linked with the ANC. A 'Release Mandela' campaign was launched which was widely supported both at home and abroad.

**SOURCE B**

*An illegal protest being made by ANC members, calling for the release of Nelson Mandela.*

**SOURCE C**

UDF UNITES - APARTHEID DIVIDES

UDF

UNITED DEMOCRATIC FRONT
FORWARD TO PEOPLES' POWER!

*A poster produced for the launch of the UDF in August 1983.*

## Worldwide opposition grows

The media began to show footage of clashes between police and protesters on television screens throughout the world. The government was constantly criticised by people who were outraged by what they saw.

## Women protest

Women began to organise and demand better treatment and wages.

## The Congress of South African Trade Unions

A great boost was given to the union movement when, in 1985, the Congress of South African Trade Unions (COSATU) was launched. It represented 33 unions and some 450,000 workers. Its General Secretary, Jay Naidoo, was determined that COSATU should not only concern itself with labour issues but should fight for a democratic, non-racial South Africa.

## SOURCE D

*Stories, poems and songs were used to remind the people of their objectives, to honour their heroes and to decry their opponents.*

Tambo's voice is heard calling – let the new men and women emerge

amidst this

Botha's voice is heard calling –

tear gas, rubber bullets, Hippos and Caspirs [personnel carriers]

mow down women, children and men

While Reagan smiles

and Thatcher grins

let them,

the friendship presents they give the Boers

are death makers for us

let them be friends

*A Tough Tale* by Mongane Serote quoted in *Beyond the Barricades*

## SOURCE E

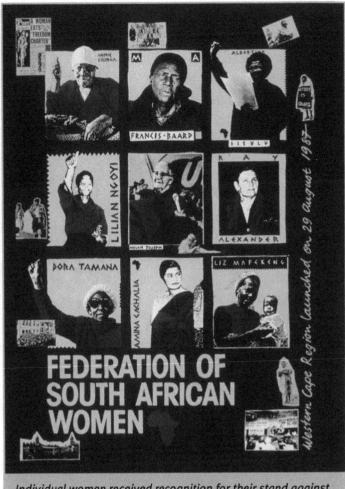

*Individual women received recognition for their stand against apartheid in this poster launched in 1987.*

## SOURCE F

*Archbishop Desmond Tutu was a leading anti-apartheid campaigner who advocated a non-violent approach to securing change in South Africa.*

## A decade of defiance

The 1980s was a time of many funerals – the funerals of people who died at the hands of the police, vigilantes and rival political groups. Hundreds, sometimes thousands of people attended the funerals. On many occasions violence erupted at the graveside and added more death to the occasion.

The anti-apartheid movements were beginning to make the country ungovernable. The government began to look more and more powerless as youths took control of the ghetto streets. People suspected of breaking boycotts or collaborating with the authorities were hunted down. Trials were held, sometimes, in hastily convened 'people's courts', and a death sentence would be quickly carried out. In some cases people would be executed by means of 'the necklace' – a burning tyre filled with petrol placed around the neck. Clashes between the Inkatha supporters of Buthelezi and members of the UDF, especially in Natal, were becoming more frequent and this added to the death toll.

**SOURCE H**

### INKATHA FREEDOM PARTY (IFP)

The Inkatha party is another important political party, whose support base is largely limited to rural Zulu peoples of KwaZulu–Natal. It was founded in 1975 as a cultural organisation by Chief Mangosuthu Buthelezi *(left)*, then an ANC member. Chief Buthelezi is the uncle of the Zulu king and a Buthelezi has traditionally served the king as Prime Minister. He accepted autonomy for his region but refused to accept 'homeland independence' from the apartheid government. But, contrary to the policy of the liberation parties, he favoured overseas investment in South Africa. Inkatha became a political party in 1990. It captured the majority of KwaZulu–Natal votes in the 1994 election. Its share of the total vote cast was 10.5 per cent.

**SOURCE G**

*Funeral of youths killed by police.*

**SOURCE I**

*Crowds protesting in 1986 about the thousands of people being arrested and the level of police brutality.*

## The reaction of the state

The government was shaken by the continuing violence, but it was by no means broken. In the first eight months of 1985 the government struck back. Around 8,000 people were detained. Many more were charged with various offences and later released. The following year another 26,000 people were detained. In a sinister development, plain-clothed undercover groups began to enter the urban ghettos at night and kill people at random. Violence became part of everyday life. Attacks could take place at home, in a train or a taxi – nowhere was safe.

## The new Prime Minister, F. W. de Klerk

In 1989, Botha, now suffering from ill health, was persuaded to step down and make way for a younger man. The opposition to his Total Strategy policy had meant that it had failed. His successor, F. W. de Klerk, would take another direction and would surprise both the nation and the world.

## >> Activity

1 How did P.W. Botha attempt to deal with the growing pressure on the government from both inside and outside the country? How successful was he?

2 What do you understand by:

FOSATU

CUSA

BAWU

COSATU?

Why were organisations such as these important in the fight against apartheid?

# Change at last

The whites-only elections held later in 1989 did not show that there was a clear majority of voters wanting change. Even so, de Klerk chose to treat the result as a mandate for reform. On 2 February 1990, in a historic speech before Parliament, he announced that the ban on the ANC, the PAC, and the South African Communist Party (SACP) would be lifted. He promised that hundreds of political prisoners would be released, including Nelson Mandela, and said that he was ready to work with all political groups.

## Negotiations for Mandela's release

Before these dramatic announcements were made there had been secret negotiations between the Minister of Justice, K. Coetsee, Prime Minister P. W. Botha and Nelson Mandela. They had met in 1985 when Mandela was recovering from an operation. Their first meeting had been informal. Politics were not discussed, but Mandela had been moved from the harsh environment of Robben Island Prison to the Pollsmoor Prison in Cape Town. It would be easier to continue the negotiations there.

Mandela was then allowed to receive visitors from outside South Africa. In 1986 a meeting was arranged between him and representatives from the Commonwealth. While the

Commonwealth representatives were in the country, South African commandos attacked ANC bases in the neighbouring territories. The disillusioned representatives left, recommending sanctions against South Africa. Mandela asked to see Botha, but his request was turned down. Other members of the government, however, continued to meet with him on a regular basis. In reality, negotiations had started.

In August 1988 Mandela became ill. When he recovered he was moved to another prison. The usual prison restrictions were lifted. He was taken out for walks and motor-car rides. No one recognised the elderly man who had become the country's most famous prisoner. He was, by now, an unusual prisoner – he had been given the key to the back door of the house in which he was living, so that he could step onto the patio which overlooked the swimming pool whenever he wished.

By July 1989 Botha was again prepared to meet Mandela in secret. It was a courtesy meeting and nothing of any political importance was discussed. But, behind the scenes, representatives from the Broederbond, big business, the UDF and the liberation movements were preparing for political change. Mandela insisted that the first step should be the release of Walter Sisulu and five other ANC prisoners. When he himself was released, the tough bargaining began.

Nelson Mandela, released after 27 years, walks to freedom with his wife, Winnie.

## Convention for a Democratic South Africa

The government began to abolish the laws that upheld discrimination. In 1991, the Convention for a Democratic South Africa (CODESA) was held. This was the most representative gathering of people that had ever met together in South Africa. The delegates found that there were no easy solutions. The PAC withdrew from the negotiations. CODESA I was followed by CODESA II which also failed to achieve any significant breakthrough. The parties to the negotiations wanted very different things and the talks faltered.

## The 1992 Referendum

Early in 1992, de Klerk held a referendum amongst the whites to find out how much support he had for the continuation of negotiations. He received the support of 70 per cent of those who

The day after the massacre of 49 people in a night attack on Boipatong, police opened fire on a protesting crowd of residents, and more people were killed. A policeman is seen here dealing violently with a member of the protesting crowd.

participated in the referendum. This encouraging signal, however, did not prevent negotiations from breaking down in the middle of 1992. The militants in the ANC felt the time had come for a show of strength. They launched a programme of 'rolling mass action', that is, continuous strikes, boycotts and street demonstrations.

## The massacre of Boipatong

On 17 June, in a black settlement called Boipatong, 49 men, women and children were massacred. Survivors described how they were attacked in the middle of the night by Zulu-speaking people; some said that whites were also involved. The population was convinced that the attack had been secretly provoked by the police. De Klerk tried to visit the area but was driven out by its furious residents. Two hours later nervous policemen opened fire on a protesting crowd, and more people died. The ANC immediately withdrew from negotiations and handed in a list of demands to the government.

## The march on Ciskei

Tens of thousands of supporters of the ANC/SACP took part in a peaceful march on Bisho, capital town of the Ciskei 'homeland'. The homeland leader, Oupa Gqozo, was unpopular and the ANC hoped that they could win over the Ciskei troops and police to their cause. Oupa Gqozo warned that he would oppose them with force. When the protesters defied an injunction to stay away from Bisho, Ciskeian soldiers opened fire. They killed 28 marchers and 200 were wounded.

Mourners at the funeral of some of those killed at Boipatong call for de Klerk to resign. At this funeral in Everton, a nearby village, a parent and child are buried together.

## The Record of Understanding

For a while it looked as if the country might collapse into anarchy, but Mandela and de Klerk recognised that the problems could only be solved if they worked together. They began to look for a way out. Joe Slovo, who had been the leader of the SACP for many years, suggested that the ANC and the National Party share power for five years. In September, the parties signed the Record of Understanding in which they agreed to renew negotiations. Buthelezi pulled his Inkatha out of the process. Disturbing talk of civil war became widespread.

## The assassination of Chris Hani

Another blow came a month later when Chris Hani, the newly appointed head of the SACP, was assassinated outside his home. Mandela appeared on television with an appeal for calm – he had become in many ways the real leader of the country. Over 100,000 people attended the funeral service for Hani and 20,000 mourners followed the coffin to the cemetery. Despite a few incidents, the wide-scale violence that had been feared did not materialise.

*Nelson Mandela and F. W. de Klerk receive the Nobel Peace Prize in December 1993.*

## Right-wing reaction

Shortly after these dramatic events, the Afrikaner Resistance Movement (AWB) stormed the World Trade Centre, where the negotiations were taking place. They shouted abuse, threatened to kill all the black delegates, and vandalised the centre.

## Sufficient consensus

Amidst the drama and tragedy, the negotiations achieved their aim. Observers gave special credit to Joe Slovo of the SACP, Cyril Ramaphosa of the ANC and Roelf Meyer of the National Party for their determined effort to make negotiations work. De Klerk and Mandela, though frequently at odds, set an example of what could be achieved. On 18 November 1993, after eight years of both formal and informal talks, an Interim Constitution for South Africa finally emerged. Its purpose was to set up a united democratic state with strong federal features. The apartheid era was over.

*Supporters demonstrating against the murder of Chris Hani.*

## The Interim Constitution

The agreement allowed for national and provincial governments; a multi-party cabinet to serve for five years; a Bill of Rights to protect minorities and a constitutional court to safeguard the future constitution. Private enterprise would be encouraged, but the government would reserve the right to intervene in the economy if it felt that it was necessary. A new defence force would be set up that would include members of the former South African Defence Force and members of the military wings of the various liberation movements.

## The elections

South Africa held its first democratic election in April 1994. On 10 May 1994, Nelson Rolihlahla Mandela, the first black South African President, was sworn into office at a ceremony attended by dignitaries from all over the world. The long march to freedom had ended.

## Discussion points

> What do you think were the most important factors that made a negotiated settlement possible?

> Why do you think the ANC won the election?

## THE ELECTION RESULTS

| Party | Votes | % | Nat. Assembly seats |
|---|---|---|---|
| African National Congress | 12 237 655 | 62.65 | 252 |
| National Party | 3 983 690 | 20.39 | 82 |
| Inkatha Freedom Party | 2 058 294 | 10.54 | 43 |
| Freedom Front | 424 555 | 2.17 | 9 |
| Democratic Party | 338 426 | 1.73 | 7 |
| Pan Africanist Congress | 243 478 | 1.25 | 5 |
| African Christian Dem. Party | 88 104 | 0.45 | 2 |

*Supporters of Nelson Mandela celebrate the election results.*

## THE RESULTS OF THE 1994 ELECTION

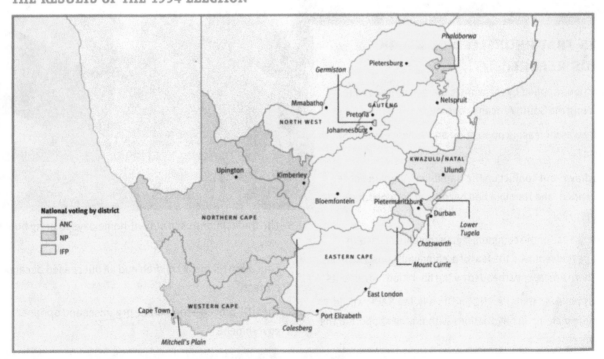

63

# The end of apartheid

## ANTI-APARTHEID PROTEST GAINS IN STRENGTH

> In the 1960s pressure groups around the world were set up to organise demonstrations and press for trade and sporting boycotts of South Africa.

> Throughout the 1960s, the newly independent black nations in Africa began to join the United Nations. Consequently the organisation became increasingly critical of South Africa's apartheid policy.

> In 1963, the new Organisation of African Unity made the abolition of apartheid in South Africa one of its main aims. Its policy was clearly set out in the Lusaka Manifesto of 1969.

> South Africa lost the support of friendly white governments along its borders as these countries gained their independence.

> South Africa's action in supporting Ian Smith and supplying him with goods during the boycott after UDI caused widespread criticism.

> South Africa's actions in South West Africa before independence was granted in 1989 were widely condemned.

## STEPS LEADING TO NEGOTIATION

> The unions were legalised

> Job reservation weakened

> The Tri-cameral Parliament was set up

> Secret negotiations

> ANC, SACP, PAC unbanned

> Political prisoners were released

### Constitution of the republic of South Africa

The new constitution, which became law in 1996, begins with these words:

We, the people of South Africa, Recognise the injustices of our past; Honour those who suffered for justice and freedom in our land; Respect those who have wanted to build and develop our country and we therefore, through our freely elected representatives, adopt this constitution as the supreme law of the republic.

*Nelson Mandela takes the oath of office at the Union Building.*

## FACTORS THAT PROPELLED DE KLERK TOWARDS REFORM

1 Sanctions applied by the world's major countries were crippling the South African economy.

2 There was increasing opposition and violence within South Africa.

3 The drawn-out conflict on the Namibian/Angolan border had ended, and Namibia had become an independent state (1989).

4 The collapse of the communist governments of Eastern Europe had removed the fear of a 'communist onslaught' in southern Africa, spearheaded by the liberation movements.

5 It was believed that the ANC and its ally, the SACP, would be more yielding in negotiations without the support of the communist bloc.

6 The trade unions used stay-at-home days to bring home their views.

7 Education for black children had all but ceased because of protest.

8 The UDF proved a formidable organiser and opponent of government.

# Index

CPSIA information can be obtained
at www.ICGtesting.com
Printed in the USA
LVHW06s1950171018
593968LV00003B/3/P